HEARTS NOT GARMENTS

HEARTS NOT GARMENTS

Christ is Our Peace

Michael Hollings

Darton, Longman and Todd
London

First published in 1982
Darton, Longman and Todd Ltd
89 Lillie Road
London SW6 1UD

© Michael Hollings 1982

ISBN 0 232 51539 5

British Library Cataloguing in Publication Data

Hollings, Michael
  Hearts not garments.
  1. Prayer
  I. Title
  248.3'2   BV210.2

  ISBN 0–232–51539–5

Phototypeset by Input Typesetting Ltd,
London SW19 8DR
Printed in Great Britain by
Richard Clay (The Chaucer Press) Ltd
Bungay, Suffolk

'Yet even now', says the Lord,
'return to me with all your heart,
with fasting, with weeping, and with mourning;
and rend your hearts and not your garments.'
Return to the Lord, your God,
for he is gracious and merciful,
slow to anger, and abounding in
steadfast love.

(Joel 2:12–13)

CHRIST IS OUR PEACE

This book is the first of a series of three focusing on Catholic Renewal in the Church of England using the central theme 'Christ is Our Peace'. This volume deals with renewal of the Christian; the remaining volumes will cover the renewal of the Church and the renewal of the world. It is hoped that the books will be read by all Christians interested in renewal, regardless of denomination.

Author's Note

I suggested that the cover should show St Francis doing what Christ asked him when he said, 'Build up my Church'. This book is published during the eight-hundredth anniversary of St Francis's birth, and in an outstanding way St Francis has always been a Christian able to unite the variety of Christian thinkers.

Michael Hollings

CONTENTS

ACKNOWLEDGEMENTS

It is not easy for me to settle down to write a book.

Things seem to happen, people happen, life is full. I therefore rely inordinately upon others who can supply some order and coherence to my thought, and unravel the sentences I put on paper, so that readers may be better able to understand what I am trying to say.

I am deeply grateful to Anthony Baxter who has gone through the whole manuscript. His keen eye and scholarship have saved me from many an error; his sensitivity has much improved the content of the book.

Living in the inner city, I find it difficult to get consecutive sentences written down without a telephone ringing, the doorbell going, or someone asking either profound moral/theological/social questions, or, as for example happened today, wanting me to arrange the fumigation of a flat which Task Force was decorating, because the decorators had all been bitten by fleas and refused to continue! Hence my gratitude to Rowley and Etta Gullick who opened the beauty of their Isle of Man home to me, giving me hospitality and time and space to get the main work of writing done in peace.

Finally, the steady typing of Sister Joe and her gentle but persuasive prodding have enabled the book to emerge.

Faults and shallowness are mine. But we must each live in the hope of transfiguration.

Michael Hollings
6 August 1981
Feast of the Transfiguration

The Scripture quotations in this publication are from the Revised Standard Version of the Bible copyrighted 1971 and 1952 by the Division of Christian Education of the National Council of the Churches of Christ in the USA.

INTRODUCTION

When I was asked to write something on Catholic Renewal in the Church of England, I was astonished. As a Roman Catholic priest, I wondered what right I had to put together anything as an offering to members of the Church of England. This was the more true since I am myself not involved in what is sometimes called Catholic Renewal in the Roman Catholic Church.

However, I came to understand that there might be considerable use, for we are all led by the same Spirit who will guide us into all truth (cf. John 16:13). This opening up enables us to share each other's insights, to criticize constructively each other's failings, and so to build together: 'Rather, speaking the truth in love, we are to grow up in every way into him who is the head, into Christ, from whom the whole body, joined and knit together by every joint with which it is supplied, when each part is working properly, makes bodily growth and upbuilds itself in love' (Eph. 4:15–16).

In the whole Church of Christ, which has been so often and so painfully rent with dissension and even bloody fratricide, we need to share everything in Christ and in the Church, so that we do indeed build up in love.

It is not uncommon in the business world of today that an individual or firm is brought in from outside to look at the affairs of a firm, in order to recommend improvements in performance. I hardly see myself in that guise, but there is a slight similarity.

I have found often in my personal ministry as a pastor that I do my best to convey the truths of Christ, the simple, rich and often stark message of the gospel to the people with whom I am committed to build up the body . . . and quite normally, there is very little apparent success. I have then stood and listened to the message of a visiting preacher who, to my mind, was reiterating the message

1

I had already proclaimed. To my surprise, and annoyance, I have afterwards been approached by a regular member of the congregation, who has been enthusiastic at this new message, saying: 'Father, why have you never told us that before?'!

Is it not also true that members of a family are frequently the last people with whom other members of the family will share; and true that parents get frustrated at their inability to touch their growing children, while now and then a distant relative or a teacher seems more able to talk with them and penetrate? It is not quite that familiarity breeds contempt. Here familiarity breeds a switch-off, a deafness, and impenetrability.

So what follows may well be criticized as containing nothing new, nothing that has not been written and said a thousand times before. But it is equally true that there is no new revelation after Christ, only a deepening, expanding awareness and insight into the deeper meaning within the word of God. In this case, for what they are worth, the following pages are my own insights, sparked from inside myself, but sparked also by a sharing with others who have helped to jog my mind, melt my heart and focus my vision. The value of these insights you have to assess, because this book is meant for reading, but meant also to be followed by discussion, out of which may emerge disagreement or agreement, qualified assent or entirely different insights. That it should stimulate is what I would ask.

I sometimes wonder how I have come to know this or that, to have certain views on life, politics, religion and so on. At other times there is an inner conviction which it is impossible to disguise, but also impossible to substantiate or make respectable rationally. I have never been much of a theologian or a scholar. My life has been spent with God and with people, but always at a pastoral level. Even when I spent eleven years in the atmosphere of Oxford University, my concern was with the growth of the undergraduates and graduates in life as a whole—life which embraces the physical, the intellectual, the romantic and the spiritual.

One reviewer of a book I wrote on the priesthood said of me something to the effect that 'he is too busy to be a radical'. I think I get his meaning, and I would agree. Nevertheless, the stuff which makes up my life and the text of this book has radically changed me from a non-believer to a believer; from a conservative accepter of what the theological college taught at the end of the nineteen-

2

forties to a person who is often thought 'dangerous' by the 'establishment' of the Roman Catholic Church. Oddly, this is partly true because as I see myself, there is in me a strange combination of the evangelical and of radical thinking and acting. This often confuses me, and must be most confusing to others!

It is enough here to say that my expressed thoughts are expected to challenge you, to ask you to think again and ever more deeply, to look at your life and your life-style, to place yourself firmly under the guidance of the Holy Spirit in the Church—and to be prepared for change of mind, heart and vision. This I cannot induce by myself, I rely upon the Holy Spirit. But I put the possibility before you in a way which is practical and down to earth.

The peace of Christ is not a drug. His peace is real, alive and active, yet still and deep and contemplative—a paradox. It is demanding: 'For the word of God is living and active, sharper than any two-edged sword, piercing to the division of soul and spirit, of joints and marrow, and discerning the thoughts and intentions of the heart' (Hebrews 4:12).

Catholic Renewal

Before continuing to the main chapters of this book, it is necessary in my mind to clarify some notions.

In a booklet entitled: *What is Catholic Renewal in the Church of England?* there is the following definition:

Catholic Renewal is a movement within the Church of England which proclaims the Catholic Faith. Catholic means 'whole', 'world-wide', the whole faith and not just those bits which the fashions of an age find acceptable; its opposite is narrow, partial, sectarian. It is the faith in Jesus Christ, proclaimed by the apostles and fathers of the Church throughout the ages. To be Catholic means to believe that God is revealed in Holy Scripture and to preach the Gospel of salvation through Jesus. To be Catholic is to believe that God is present in his Church and that his grace is given through the Sacraments.

Catholic Renewal is not an organisation; there are no subscription lists, no membership cards; anyone can become part of it who loves the Lord Jesus. It is not a group of people who prefer 'high Church' liturgy; it is not a group of people who wish that they were Roman Catholics; it is a body of Christians who are working for the unity of the Church which Jesus Christ founded, East and West, that the world may believe.

The word 'Catholic' which is present in the Creed of belief of Christians is used by different views of Christianity in different ways. To my mind, it includes all that is basic in Scripture, together with later insights in the tradition which are in conformity with the Scripture. To say that, is to open up and then beg the issues. I cannot do more than that here, but you must take it that this principle is behind what I write.

The word 'Catholic' envisages the unity among Christians stated by St Paul: 'eager to maintain the unity of the Spirit in the bond of peace. There is one body and one Spirit, just as you were called to the one hope that belongs to your call, one Lord, one faith, one baptism, one God and Father of us all, who is above all and through all and in all' (Eph. 4:3–6). This is certainly not visible today. One of the greatest stumbling blocks to such unity is the sort of 'uniformity' which may be demanded by any one section of believing Christians; and this raises the question of how uniform has that belief ever been, when, beneath an agreed formula, an individual is questioned about his or her mental clarity, verbal doctrinal conformity, and spiritual realization?

The word 'Renewal' is also complicated. It has been taken over by certain sections. Some envisage a kind of 'back-to-the-land', Garden of Eden, concept where all things are bright and beautiful as they were initially set up by God to be—a first stage in God's plan which was perfect till mankind spoiled it. There is an element which takes renewal to mean charismatic renewal; and which goes all out for openness to the Spirit, much group work, in prayer especially, and a sense of exclusiveness, not unlike the fundamentalist: 'Have you been saved?, for which is substituted: 'Have you received the Spirit?'

Now I want to make it quite clear that I do not see from my viewpoint anything which is exclusive, or which says this is a movement which has to be joined in a narrow sense. The movement is the movement of the Spirit of God, working in the Church and the world, moving where the Spirit wills, unconfined, untrammelled, free. This is the breath of the Spirit poured out, not turned on like a tap at man's whim. Least of all is this 'renewing' in the sense of recapturing something which has been lost.

Therefore, while accepting the use of the term 'renewal' as expressive of something which is felt to be a fresh vision and life in the Church and especially in the people of the Church, I want to stress that my understanding is in line with the words of St Paul: 'Therefore, if anyone is in Christ, he is a new creation; the old has passed away, behold, the new has come. All this is from God, who through Christ reconciled us to himself and gave us the ministry of reconciliation; that is, God was in Christ reconciling the world to himself, not counting their trespasses against them, and entrusting to us the message of reconciliation. So we are ambassadors for Christ, God making his appeal through us. We beseech you on behalf of Christ, be reconciled to God' (2 Cor. 5:17–20).

We are already sharers in the new creation in Christ. What has to be freshened up in us by the power of the Spirit is the realization—the making real of this new life, because for many of us the life has itself become stale, without salt, without savour; and consequently not only have we suffered depression and a sense of defeatism, but those others for whom we are to be ambassadors have caught our uncertainty rather than our conviction, our irrelevance rather than Christ's saving power.

The involvement in what is called Catholic Renewal therefore is the involvement of each of us individually and all of us collectively in a deepening relationship with Jesus Christ. This must be a real living experience which flows from prayer, Scripture, Eucharist, reconciliation and service in God's world through union in the Church. This will involve myself, home, work, the local community and the wider world.

It is in a simple way summed up in Jesus' repeated call: 'Follow me.' But it is not an easy call, and it should not leave time to be titillated by frills or involved in controversies about the shape of vestments or the number of candles on the altar. . . , all that used to be included in the phrase 'smells and bells', and still lingers on in more congregations than I would care to number. The issues of salvation are not in these things; such things are not the issues of the gospel, of relationship with God; nor are they the concern of a starving world, a violent world and an unemployed world. To put

5

them forward in priority is to devalue Christianity not only for ourselves, but for those to whom we are ambassadors.

But deepened relationship with Jesus Christ implies deepened relationship with yourself. This results from the Spirit of Jesus working in you, and this will in turn make demands upon you in your way of living. Renewal is costly, not cosy; renewal is an opening vision of God and his world, not pulling up the drawbridge against increasing secularization; renewal is a going out into the world to witness among all nations. Renewal holds together in tension the cross and the resurrection. It is not a small clique of like-minded kindred, but the whole variety of the people of God, whom Jesus loves.

Therefore, we shall find that Christ is our peace not by running away, but by facing up to; not by compromising but by the compassion of Christ; not by stopping in fear but by going ahead in hope. We shall find nothing can ever be quite the same again, even our knowledge of God's love. We shall be asked to die in many ways we considered vital, and to live in many ways we had not conceived before. All this is God's work, and he working in us 'is able to do far more abundantly than all that we ask or think' (Eph. 3:20). Then we can live the paradox of movement and stability, the beauty ever old and ever new:

> Thou dost keep him in perfect peace,
> whose mind is stayed on thee,
> because he trusts in thee.
> Trust in the Lord for ever,
> for the Lord God
> is an everlasting rock. (Isaiah 26:3–4)

A broader purpose
There is one footnote to this introduction. Though intended for study within the Church of England, it is my hope that others will find substance in this book either of interest, encouragement or controversy. The more dialogue and cross-fertilization there is at all levels of churchmanship across the Christian denominations, the more hope there will be for progressively more positive union of faith and love and service.

Once again, this will call for change, movement, hard work and ever deeper commitment in love.

Chapter 1

GOD KNOWLEDGE—SELF-KNOWLEDGE

Know yourself

During eleven years as chaplain to Roman Catholics at Oxford University, I went each summer to spend time sharing a Borstal experience. A group of undergraduates joined a group of lads from a particular Borstal institution. A week was spent in camp in Yorkshire, a week back in the institution itself. Senior support came from chaplains and a camp commandant, normally from the University.

Over the years, I worked mainly with two college chaplains. One is now Bishop of Chichester, the other Bishop of Newcastle. I vividly remember my first visit with the latter to Hewell Grange Borstal, near Redditch. We went together into the chapel. On the wall behind the altar in staring capital letters was inscribed: KNOW YOURSELF.

I commented at the time that this would put me off every time I came into the chapel, but interestingly that phrase which I had known before came to mean much more from that time onwards.

In theory, the Borstal system was devised as a learning experience, not merely a punitive imprisonment. For one reason or another, lads there had fallen foul of the law. Often this originated from a deprived background, a broken family, a loveless childhood, a mixed-up personality. Just as Christian life is meant to be a growing in wisdom and grace and God's favour (cf. Luke 2:40), so relation with oneself, with God and with others was meant to be part of the Borstal training. Unfortunately, as with Christianity as it is lived, the success rate did not seem very good. It was often painfully obvious that the boys' failure in relationship in themselves and with others at an earlier stage of childhood and adolescence was difficult to put right. It is easier to scar or break than it is to heal. The young men's misery often erupted after discharge.

But for me, to be there with them was to learn to know myself better. In that closed situation I found myself afraid. I suffered a sense of depersonalization, was angry at the system, felt unfounded and harmful superiority which quickly led to being patronizing.

This links for me with the exercise we are now engaged in. Know yourself is at the foundation if we are to be liberated, but that very knowledge implies sloughing off certain attitudes, being converted to new ideas and ways. All too easily we can come to live a routine Christianity according to law, and fail to penetrate to the spirit. The routine of saying prayers, churchgoing, church committees and so on has a deadening effect on the spiritual life. It brings to mind St Paul's words: 'Likewise, my brethren, you have died to the law through the body of Christ, so that you may belong to another, to him who has been raised from the dead in order that we may bear fruit for God. . . . Now we are discharged from the law, dead to that which held us captive, so that we serve not under the old written code but in the new life of the Spirit' (Romans 7:4, 6).

St Paul is not discarding the law, but insisting on the need of Christ to fulfil the law, because of the depth of our unspiritual part. For me, it is only possible to get this into perspective, to be deepened, if we follow the long-standing Catholic tradition of stillness, prayer, meditation and contemplation. The Catholic tradition is not all *doing*. It is also *hearing*: 'My mother and my brothers are those who hear the word of God and do it' (Luke 8:21). 'Blessed rather are those who hear the word of God and keep it' (Luke 11:28).

There is no beginning, no way forward, no newness of spiritual purpose, which is not based upon a solid knowledge of self gained partly in silent stillness. To this must be intimately linked knowledge of Jesus Christ. Without knowledge of yourself, you cannot truly love yourself. Without knowledge of Jesus Christ, your love will always lack a dimension. To be true love, knowledge must be true. That is not to say that limited love is not possible and often found. The love Jesus speaks of and leads us to is beyond such limit because it is the love of God.

The need to pause and review life, to give time for the word and love of God to penetrate, is paramount. We can easily deceive ourselves, or be deceived. If this is so, then we have to ask ourselves whether we are sufficiently deeply founded on these two knowledges, of ourselves and Jesus Christ. If these knowledges are insufficient,

10

so our adherence to and life in the Church will be insufficient for us to grow 'to mature manhood, to the measure of the stature of the fullness of Christ' (Eph. 4:13).

It is the task of each one of us, where possible with the help of another person, to face these questions and live out the truth of the answers.

The two knowledges come firstly from prayer and study of the Gospels, secondly from people and the world. But it is important that the way forward into knowledge is not undertaken as a self-indulgence, in order to become one of the élite. It will only be truly valuable and honest work if it is done for the threefold love expressed in the Scriptures—love of God, love of yourself, love of your neighbour. All three interconnect and are equally important. They are often thought about, talked about, preached about. Yet it is difficult to live out a balance. At least one element of the triangle of love is often neglected, or at least weaker than the other two.

The above quotation from Romans speaks of making us 'fruitful for God'. The area of examination we are on is this very newness or renewal which should make us fruitful for God. If we think we are already part of that Catholic Renewal, is it making us fruitful for God? If we are not part of it, would it make us fruitful for God? I speak and write as someone looking in on Catholic Renewal in the Church of England who is himself hoping to be fruitful for God in his own life. And the thought I put out to you is that, at present, I am not at all clear that this movement within the Church of England is in fact being fruitful for God. Generally speaking I do not see it vitalizing parishes, achieving a deepening of commitment, giving a deeper life of faith and witness to large numbers of committed church people. I may be wrong. But from your point of view, it is worth considering how you stand, because the object of thinking, praying and discussing is a very practical one. On the one hand the purpose is to assist in the deepening commitment of the 'already committed'. You know, I am sure, that with your openness to him, there is much that the Holy Spirit can and will do in this regard.

On the other hand and more importantly, if we are for God and for others rather than for ourselves, can you say that Catholic Renewal in the Church of England is becoming a beacon for the lost in their wilderness wandering, a magnet to attract the distracted attention of young people, a focus to concentrate the uncommitted

11

who find God and religion, but especially established religion, utterly irrelevant to their lives? To my mind, the signs of renewed interest—and these are patchy and not over-strong—are to be found more often among churches of an evangelical outlook, or among smaller sects or so-called 'black churches'.

In getting to know ourselves and Jesus Christ, in making an assessment in truth so that we can go forward, there is a fundamental question which needs to be asked. . . . Is there something lacking in us? Is there something lacking in the corporate expression of Catholic Renewal in the Church of England at the local, parochial level, or in the national living out of renewal? It should also be asked whether there is anything lacking in the Catholic tradition of the Church of England among the individual leadership and membership—something which might drastically change the impact here and now—something which, if detected, could be so lived out that it would by the working of the Spirit make the bridge between irrelevance and the power of the Good News of Jesus Christ.

I give you a serious pointer from the church world of fifty years ago. Consider if this strikes a chord with you today.

The Gap
Dom Bede Frost of Nashdom wrote in 1931:

Anyone who is at all familiar with the present position of Catholicism in the Anglican Communion—that is, in any or all of the provinces in communion with the see of Canterbury—must be conscious of a certain 'gap' in teaching and practice which, to a much larger extent than is generally recognised, nullifies and renders sterile all the considerable progress which has been, and is being, made.

That 'gap' is the absence of insistence upon, and the practice of, mental prayer. . . .

We have seen, almost within the limits of a lifetime, the recovery of Catholic ideals, faith and practice in a country which more than any other had lost touch with the main stream of Catholic tradition and life; we have familiarised the people of England, as no one else could have done, with doctrines they had forgotten, Sacraments they ignored, and practices they had been taught to

12

abhor: we have got an appreciable number of them to Mass and the Sacraments and to some growing perception of the supernatural, yet we are, or should be, sadly conscious that something is yet lacking. There is; and it is the realisation of the fact that the acceptance of the Faith, the hearing of Mass and the reception of the Sacraments are not all; that Faith, Cultus and Sacraments need a background and reinforcing power. That background, that power, is the interior life of prayer.

(Dom Bede Frost, *The Art of Mental Prayer* Philip Allen 1931, pp. 3–5)

Today many parts of the world have moved on much more deeply into secularization. Practice of religion has fallen away: God-Knowledge in any real sense is scattered and localized and often itself secularized. No church has any reason for complacency. Although in the seventies there has been an increased awareness of prayer, the sixties were taken up with good works, and in the eighties commitment to personal prayer and the spiritual life is still widely discounted.

It has been my continued theme for the past thirty years that a deep life of personal prayer, together with community worship, both leading to knowledge, love and service of God, are absolutely essential for the growth of the Christian and of Christianity. My theme is the same today, and today it seems more than ever necessary to be clear that I have not changed my tune. Rather I seek further to strengthen it, especially in the face of those who put forward the notion that our salvation is worked only within history, or again who give Jesus Christ a position simply as the supreme example of humanity, without accepting him as God. I am brought back again and again to two passages in the Gospel, which link together in my thinking: 'And this is eternal life, that they know thee the only true God, and Jesus Christ whom thou hast sent' (John 17:3), and 'The kingdom of God is in the midst of you' (Luke 17:21). The way in which we work out our salvation in history should be the reality of our day-by-day living of the three loves— God, self and neighbour—but this is only real in the context of eternity as well as this world, if we accept the God-dimension. This is the Catholic tradition. What are its implications?

Making a space in life for God

The first implication, and this has to do with knowing yourself, is to decide firmly whether you are personally convinced of the necessity of personal prayer as paramount in your life. I do not mean a notional 'Yes', as anyone would react who accepted the existence of God with whom there can be some link through prayer and worship. No! I mean a conviction which is so strong that it changes the priorities and therefore the pattern of your living.

In working with a government inquiry into education, I came across a sad story of muddled priorities. A young husband and wife with one child were determined that from the start of life that child should always have one of the parents at home in his early years. Accordingly the man worked nights, the woman days. Unfortunately, it transpired that the man slept during the day, and the women came back tired and went to bed early, so that when the child came to school at the age of five, he could hardly talk!

Our relationship with God can also get wrong in priorities when we fall into what has been called the 'heresy of good works', putting doing before being. It is possible to be so busy 'about God's work' that there is no time left for God. St John of the Cross is not speaking above our capacity but very practically when he writes:

A very little of this pure love is more precious in the sight of God and the soul, and of greater profit to the Church, even though the soul appear to be doing nothing, than all these other works together. For this reason Mary Magdalene, although she wrought great good with her preaching, and would have continued to do so because of the great desire she had to please her Spouse and to profit the Church, hid herself in the desert for thirty years in order to surrender herself truly to this love, since it seemed to her that in every way she would gain more by so doing, because of the great profit and importance there is to the Church in a very little of this love! . . . Let those, then, that are great actives, that think to girdle the world with their outward works and their preachings, take note here that they would bring far more profit to the Church and be far more pleasing to God (apart from the good example which they would give of themselves) if they spent only half as much time in abiding with God in prayer, even if they had not reached such a height as this.

(Allison Peers, ed., *Spiritual Canticle* Anthony Clarke 1978, second redaction, annotation for stanza 29)

14

Particularly in England and in the post-Reformation Church there has been a special emphasis on activity for God, and the idea of monks and nuns shutting themselves away from the world in order to give themselves to loving contemplation is often seen as a waste. Much of this has to do with the concept of God. If God is considered impersonally, and indeed spoken of only in such non-personal terms as 'ground of our being', it is very difficult to speak in such terms as love. Yet the precedent and the Catholic tradition which has come through Scripture and the earliest and continuing teaching of the Church is very much in personal terms.

Much thinking and writing in theological circles seems to me to minimize the spiritual or the transcendent, so that the God-seeker is kept within rational limits, working away at the tangible in this world, and unwilling to admit the whole realm of spiritual reality which goes beyond the world of the mind, beyond the arguments of philosophy, beyond words to the Word. While I would agree that much spiritual writing has been produced which can be demolished rationally, I am none the less convinced of the world beyond this world, of the God who is of course the ground of our being, but is not the ground of our being just in the world as we know it, but also beyond our knowledge.

If theologians succeed in reducing God to an understandable entity, they will only satisfy themselves at the more surface level of the human mind and reduce the human potential in their reduction of God. If those who travel the way in the Catholic tradition go along with this, they will cease being Catholic. However, this does not mean that the theological work now being done is unnecessary or to be ignored. It is very much part of the world in which Jesus Christ lived once as earthly man, and lives now in the Spirit. It should be the care of the Christian to know what is being thought and taught, so that the insights may be absorbed, and the areas which seem incompatible with right doctrine studied and prayed over and put into perspective. In Catholic tradition mystery will always remain.

Part of the essence of a renewed approach to God is to maintain the priority of prayer. In itself, prayer can be put on one side today for fear of seeming ridiculous, or through genuine conversion away from the personal God who relates to mankind personally. You can see that, if you are not yourself convinced of the possibility and priority of prayer, you can easily drop the notion as outmoded.

Some of the reason for an acceptance of work as the only true prayer is that true personal prayer to and with the true personal God is really a labour of love. Much of it remains mysterious, intangible, dark. Most spiritual writers stress that this sense of labouring and catching nothing is the lead temptation for beginners in prayer. . . ; and remember many of us stay beginners over many years.

St Teresa of Avila, who was so close to St John of the Cross in her spiritual outlook, uses as an example the drawing of water from a well by use of a rope. She likens the prayer of a beginner to a person lowering a single bucket, and only getting up a little water after a long and tedious haul. Given the crowded, busy lives many lead today, we can easily and quickly reach a point when the labour, the boredom and the lack of 'success' turn us away as a waste of valuable time, when we could be *doing* something. But St Teresa, who herself spent some twenty years before her break-through to God, urges us to persevere, and encourages the beginner with the hope that after all this striving and achieving only a little water in the bucket, there will come a time when the ordinary rope seems suddenly to have been superseded by a windlass. After this, far less toil is needed, and the soul is watered much more lavishly, because now it is God who is doing the work.

The simple message is: Do not give up; do not despair; do not be tempted to think it all a waste of time. Humanly speaking it may be a waste of time, but then how much time have you wasted on waiting for someone you think you love? And there is no one better to waste time on than God. You may think you will have all eternity to love him, and could here and now be better employed doing a good work. But again, the simple message which God speaks is the paradox that if you give him more time, you will have more for other work.

Regularity in prayer

The second implication is that, if you conclude that prayer really is of the essence of your Christianity, then you will have to rearrange your life. You will have to make a proper space for God, so that out of that well of time given to him there will flow the living water

16

which will fertilize and encourage spiritual growth throughout all your living.

Is there then any measure of the amount of time as such? The very ancient tradition, from the time of Moses anyhow, was that we keep the sabbath holy. This has largely gone out of fashion and so out of practice. Even with shorter working weeks, we seem if anything busier than ever. The ancient rule also made space for prayer inside each day, so that lasting Catholic teaching was that at least there should be prayer for every Christian in the morning and at night. Looking back through history, there was probably a greater sense of the atmosphere of prayer being about in a day when we were less urbanized, a sense which still remains in some rural areas, and in the lives of certain clergy, monks and nuns, more than in many families. Is it significant that those who continue to practise prayer through the day are not Christian, but for instance the Hindu and the Moslem?

To underline this, and then to bring it back to Christianity and to ourselves, reflect upon the encounter of a man with a swami in Malaysia—a man who subsequently became a Benedictine monk:

Every week for about eighteen months, I went out to this holy man of God, sat down beside him and meditated with him for half an hour. He told me that—provided I was serious in my quest—it was absolutely necessary to meditate twice a day every day. He said: Meditating only when you come out to see me will be frivolity. Meditating once a day will be frivolity. If you are serious and if you want to root this mantra in your heart, then this is the minimum undertaking . . . that you meditate first thing in the morning for half an hour and sometime in the evening for half an hour. And during the time of your meditation there must be in your mind no thoughts, no words, no imaginations. The sole sound will be the sound of your mantra, your word. [A mantra is a single word or phrase used by a person in continual repetition in prayer.] The mantra (he continued) is like a harmonic. As we sound this harmonic within ourselves we begin to build up a resonance. That resonance then leads us forward to our own wholeness. . . . We begin to experience the deep unity we all possess with our own being. And then the harmonic begins

17

to build up a resonance between you and all creatures and all creation, and a unity between you and your Creator.

I would often ask the swami: How long will this take? How long will it take me to achieve enlightenment? But the swami would either ignore my crassness or else would reply with the words that really sum up his teaching and his wisdom: Say your mantra. In those eighteen months this was the essential core of everything he had to say: Say your mantra.

(Dom John Main, *Christian Meditation*, Talk to the Cistercian Community of Gethsemani Abbey, Grail Publications 1977)

By force of the circumstances of life, there will be differences in the amount of time available for any one individual as opposed to another. A priest, monk, religious sister or wholly dedicated lay person should have life so organized that such a pattern as given by the swami would indeed be 'the minimum'. But is this true today of the thinking and living of those of us who are called to these ways of life? For others, busy men and women in home, family, work and recreation, is there a target to aim at, a basic minimum of time to be set aside—the half hour morning and evening? It is not my purpose to frighten you off, to make you feel this is all beyond you. It is not. Even a minimum of five minutes morning and evening would be a fine launching pad. The essence is not so much the length of time as the regularity.

In taking stock, in order to move forward in new life and to become 'fruitful for God', we need to think where we have stood in the past and where we stand today. Has there been growth or development, conscious or unconscious; or a falling away, as other matters invade time? In talking up and down the country, to or-dained and non-ordained, I have gathered the impression that there is quite a lot of routine praying, saying of the Offices of the Church, and regularity at worship. For the latter, numbers are perhaps greater than in past years. But time and again it is worrying to find that there is not that breadth of time-space given over to a more open prayer which is essential if deepening is to follow.

There are indeed areas of growth. Some have discovered the need for help from another person, so as to be led into new paths or ways of prayer, schools of meditation, the deeper more silent prayer. Some have found that prayer with a group of others is not so terrifying as they thought, and indeed is a freeing experience, which deepens because of sharing and feeling able to express openly the depth of what is in the heart. Others again get led to a charismatic approach that brings also a sense of liberation and a community of feeling with others, which can be a source of great joy, peace and increase in understanding of the love of God and the power of the Spirit.

However, there remain great sections of people who affirm Christianity, yet do not manage to penetrate beyond a surface realization which does not stir the inner person. Though good in itself and certainly better than nothing, the danger is that a complacency is built up, and the eyes of the spiritual person in us are blinded to the deeper demand of love, as well as to the vision of spiritual and material poverty in the world.

The way of life

Making a space in life for God and prayer radically changes the whole of that life, if it is lived out seriously. This is because prayer and setting aside a space for this specifically is an immediate way of lining up our personal will with the will of God for a short while. This is one of the natural tussles that anyone will have in getting down to pray, for it is natural that there will be a revulsion on the part of much that is human from this submission to God's will, especially when it seems so contrary to common sense and man's practicality.

Yet, if there is any shorthand definition of sanctity, it must simply be the total conforming of an individual's will to the will of God. This is learnt in the exposure of the will, co-operative and rebellious, in prayer. The effect then spills over as the will, which has in prayer learnt a little of God's will, picks up the scent during the minutes, hours and days of ordinary living:

Prayer that is worthy of the name demands total commitment, and such commitment demands of us a true and costing response. As a man sows, so shall he reap, and as a man lives, so shall he pray. Prayer and life, living and praying are indivisible. In order that contemplative prayer may be truly the bringing of the Holy Spirit into the world's pain and tensions, there must be an ele-

19

ment of costly purification. This requires positive detachment for those giving themselves seriously to the work of prayer. If prayer is learning to unite our wills with the will of God, then the cost must be the cost of Calvary. To learn to love as Christ loves is to discover through commitment the true renewing of our whole being, in God, on behalf of the world.

(Mother Mary Clare, SLG, *Encountering the Depths* DLT 1981)

It is through this practice that we become fruitful for God: because what he works in us is an increased awareness or sensitivity, which makes us more available for the burdens, sorrows and pains of the world around us. As it effects the tone of our living, something comes across to others which is beyond anything which we can cultivate ourselves. The effect of this can be both positive and negative. On the positive side, it will attract people who want to go further in God's love, people who want to know about what makes one tick, people who are in distress and need compassion and love, and often material help. On the negative side, it can rouse hostility from some who feel themselves threatened, or mockery from some who think we must be mad.

Have no doubt though that this will help you to know God better, to understand something of his will, to believe in him more deeply and personally than is portrayed in the phrase 'ground of being', to respond to what you 'know' by striving to live according to his will, according to his love. Further, through all this you will subtly come to fulfil the admonition: Know yourself.

Chapter 2

THE FAMILY

Old and New Testament could be summed up as a family history or a history of family. The ethos, atmosphere and emergence of the story of mankind from creation down to the epilogue of the Book of Revelation are the history of the family of man, created to be the family of God. Wording, thought, selection of material, moral teaching and constant reference back to God in the Old Testament narrow the family of Israel to a special place, but still encounter others living also in and from family. The New Testament further reinforces the sense of family. Jesus begins to preach and teach that God is his Father and our Father. But now the emphasis is less enclosed. Imaging the situation pictorially, Jesus speaks as the shepherd who eventually achieves one flock and sends his followers out to bring all nations to discipleship, all into the one family.

There can be no argument that the Catholic and Christian tradition has constantly laid great stress upon family from that day to this, both in regard to belonging to a human family, leading to the complicated development of marriage laws; and in regard to the family of the Church, with much emphasis upon belonging, not through birth, but through the sacrament of baptism.

In modern times, one of the greatest casualties of our society has been the family. Particularly in the large industrial complexes and urban developments there has been erosion in many directions. The increasingly high divorce rate combines with the rapid emergence of large numbers of one-parent families; the very planning of homes in our cities has taken on the nuclear family aspect of limited child-accommodation; it is now more and more common for both parents to be working, except in periods of high unemployment.

One of the urgent questions which anyone who is wanting to be fruitful for God must ask and try to solve concerns the future development of the family. Are we now in a new situation, in modern society, where the old ideas of family are outmoded, where new ideas are rightly overriding ancient family morality? Is there still a possibility of entering marriage on a permanent, lifelong basis, or are we being obtusely old-fashioned and narrow-minded if we maintain what Catholic tradition has strongly maintained down the ages and still maintains today, the unity and indissolubility of marriage?

The individual and the family

The emphasis of the last chapter was upon the individual and self-knowledge combining with knowledge of God. It is of individuals that families are made up. Each individual (this against some present day philosophies) is uniquely important as a creation of God. For this reason by itself, it is vital that the individual be encouraged to come to a knowledge and love of God.

But also, the individual is not alone. We live in the family of human beings, even if our own smaller family circle is for some reason broken. So any one individual may have a number of different 'families' within which he or she is living—human family, sports family, village family, church family, work family, political family. Some are tighter links than others. And strength of relationship within one family may strengthen or weaken relationship within another. If a man or woman is too much taken up with his sports family or his church family, or again his work family, he may neglect human family of wife and children, and so on.

Because of this pressure from society and indeed this appeal of society, there is all the more reason for the individual to be able to grow in an atmosphere which is the combination of authority and freedom, but one which is redolent of God in all its aspects of living. The spiritual which is in the human being does not simply grow in line with all other human growth; it is a strong yet tender plant; it needs fertilizing with knowledge and love. On the other hand, it is not meant to be a hot-house plant which catches a fatal dose of frost as soon as it comes into the open.

This is where the role of the family can be so decisive in its formative value. But getting a balance in family living today is a very difficult problem, and it seems to me that this should be a major concern in all pastoral work within the churches. So much of the present and the future depends upon the developing family. And by this I mean that developing which begins with the individual in himself or herself long before marriage, continues in and through marriage, and is not complete until death. But all the time, we are different age groups at different stages of development, so that it is hard to say where it is best to start these thoughts.

Baptism and the family
St Paul writes: 'Do you not know that all of us who have been baptized into Christ Jesus were baptized into his death? We were buried therefore with him by baptism into death, so that as Christ was raised from the dead by the glory of the Father, we too might walk in newness of life' (Rom. 6:3–4).

The major parts of the Christian Church have long had the practice of baptizing infants. There are notable exceptions, like the Baptists, and there are those today who suggest it would be better if baptism was given only when a person was old enough to make a personal act of faith in Jesus Christ. Rather than arguing that, because it is too far away from the present practice of today, I want to take the situation as it is, and look to see where we stand and where new vision might take us.

It is difficult to analyse the division between true faith and super-stition when a child is presented for baptism, unless there is some knowledge of the parents beforehand. In rural areas this can be comparatively easy. In the city, it may be very difficult. If it is possible to arrange that there must be some instruction of the parents before the time comes for baptism, then at the very least the person interviewing them will get some notion as to why they are there. When questioned answers vary from: 'His Gran in Italy/Ireland/West Indies says we must have him done.', to 'It's like vaccination, ain't it? Best be on the safe side.', to 'We both believe in Jesus Christ, we are both at Mass every Sunday, and we want our little Mary to be part of the family of the Church.'

If too many of those coming to present their children fall into the first two answers, we are likely to be in trouble later, unless we can devise a programme which both instructs and involves the parents beforehand, and is capable of being sustained in follow-up. Both of

23

these elements can be hard to set up and can still make little or no impact. People are free. If they are not clearly committed, we can only try to explain, encourage and seek assurance of intent to worship God. Efforts should be made, gently but firmly, to make clear the responsibility which parents are taking upon themselves as the educators of their children in the way of faith. The sacraments are not to be used as talismans or charms. They are believed in Catholic tradition to be effective of what they signify. But they are also in the hands of human beings, who have been entrusted by Jesus Christ to witness to him and bring all nations to him.

However, let us be quite clear of the dangerous situation in which we are now living. Firstly, it is difficult to refuse baptism . . . difficult immediately because of the insistence of parents and godparents: difficult in future vision, because it is hard to see that the parents will not succeed in getting a child baptized somewhere eventually, even against advice and even refusal. Difficult too in that we cannot be sure that the grace of baptism received by a child, with all the prayer and effort we put into the ceremony in addition, may not bring a new life to the parents.

Let me outline a parish situation in my experience. Here is an inner city parish, very cosmopolitan, with many different cultural backgrounds. Reviewing the children we had baptized in one year (1979–80) we found we had exactly one hundred. Looking at the marital position of their parents, we found these statistics:

> Married in church 40
> Married in the Registry Office 20
> Not married at all ....40.

In addition to that, we have to face the fact that those married in church are by no means all as alive in their belief and practice as they might be.

The Church is responsible both for the sacraments and for people. We must neither be too hard in refusing the former because of our respect and even possessiveness, nor must we be too lax from softness, and even a desire to be liked. Ministers especially have a heavy responsibility, but being in and with congregations they should be able to work out a policy which will have flexibility, but may enhance the chances of at least introducing the individual child to a small community of living faith.

Additionally to that (and bringing in the local community, the local church which is the local family) every effort should be made to let the family of the child realize that they are part of a real community. All too often, baptism is the last contact that family have with church and the community until another baptism, a funeral or wedding, or even the confirmation of the same child! And this is not Christian living, it is not really making the child part of God's family, except in a vaccination or superstitious way.

Given adult baptism, the onus of the profession of faith is all upon the person asking for baptism. With infant or child baptism, the onus is upon the parents who have asked for the baptism of their child. Whereas in days gone by there was a certain Christian presence or atmosphere from family, friends or neighbours, today, instead, many things will pull parents from practice and discourage them. Often without realizing it, the Christian family is being imbued with odd notions and even antagonistic material from the media which enter most homes, are met on the advertising hoardings in the street, and are the normal assumption in many people's lives. The local Christian community must help them in maintaining, developing and living the following of Christ, just as members of the early Church strengthened each other against persecution.

Adolescence, family and faith

While mother and father are coping with each other, learning to love in different ways and at different levels, they are also coping with the work situation and the world situation. Let no one minimize the tensions which come. At the same time, let us all take heart and wonder in admiration at the almost heroic endeavours which many families make in the most adverse conditions. We can easily be obsessed by the breakdowns and failures, when so much encouragement and joyful recognition is needed by those who persevere, and who show the rest of us the joy and strength of love shared.

At the same time, the child or children will be growing up through interesting, exciting and sometimes difficult phases of their lives, especially in adolescence. At this period of life as at others, it would be excellent if there was guidance for the parents and a support for each other in the arts of listening—of being at the same time firm

25

and flexible; the art of the way to practise the faith which is accepted, while leaving some room for manoeuvre by the younger members of the family. This is a minefield, both for priest and people, and a fair number of parents almost wash their hands in despair of having control or any relationship with their adolescent family, while others exert a pressure to keep their young people conforming.

All this points to there being a need in the Church of modern times for the members of all ages to realize we all continue as learners through our lives. This learning is again back to learning directly from our silence and our prayer and our stillness, rather than our activity. But it is also based upon a readiness to be open to the teaching of the Church, to the insights of modern knowledge, science and psychology. The question to be raised is what can be done locally by all members of the Church, but especially by those who are involved on a full-time basis, to assist, support, teach and encourage parents? What can be done to open parents to the real need they have for such assistance, when they may well say and feel that it is their problem and they don't want outside interference.

A home is to be a home. Young people need a lot of support in their growing up in the present climate. The ordinary pressures are multiplied today when against the urge to do well in the examination field is offset the gloom of unemployment as a very possible outcome to whatever is achieved at school. When there is breakdown at home, violence in the streets, the threat of nuclear war hanging in the air, is it not to be expected that growing up will be more and more difficult? And so the unity, peace and love of home is not only desirable at all levels, but an essential ingredient.

Here clearly is the challenge to a 'newness of life' in the family, which has as its keynote the difference which is made to individuals within a family, and to the family as a whole, if there is a live and loving Christian faith in the home. The old saying is, 'Prayer is caught, not taught.' This is also true of faith. In a sense, we impose our faith on children at baptism; then we are responsible for living it out, so that this may help the children to grow, and become strong, filled with wisdom (cf. Luke 2:40). For at some stage the young people *must* come to the point of possessing that faith individually, or discarding it. Faith is really both caught and taught, so that parental faith is still of vital importance at this stage. If it is a

26

faith which is absolute and brooks no discussion, it will come up against the adolescent tendency to seek independence, to question and even to reject what is parental. Undoubtedly the presentation of a strong faith can make a deep impression, especially if it is bound up with loving, caring and warmth.

It would be wrong to dismiss such strength, but its application to the growing young is one which needs also gentleness. There should be a tolerance of genuine teenage inability to believe. There should be patience with the process of personal selection. Refusal of freedom for development at this stage can be destructive both of the person and of the seed of belief. The attitude of the father in the story of the Prodigal Son is an important reference point.

On the other hand, the acceptance of the possibility of doubt and even of disbelief is an element which I find important yet dangerous. By that I mean that, having myself gone through disbelief, I know what it is like. Having come back to believing, I became pretty absolute and perhaps intolerant. Since then I have continued to pray and to live, to believe and to question. In this, I have had many years of working with teenagers from the highest to the lowest intelligence, coming from the back streets of London, Liverpool and Glasgow, as well as from castles, banks and multi-national corporation backgrounds; some too have been sons and daughters of shopkeepers, engineers, soldiers, and civil servants. A variety. . . , and a variety of faith, disbelief and questioning going across the board.

The need to accept that there will be questioning, that mankind has been given intelligence to be used and that God wants the love of free people and not the submission of slaves is to me all important. This is the value of accepting and living with the disbelief, the lack of belief or the inability to believe among young people. Whatever their commitment to believing, they are loved by God. I too should love them, and that means both wishing them well, and helping them to be fully themselves. I do not think they are harmed by knowing that I had a period of disbelief; I believe they are helped by knowing that my present belief is still something which needs the help of God, my own effort and the willingness to live with the nag of doubt which is offset by a real but inexpressible hope and trust.

I realize that I personally am detached, in the sense that these young people are not my flesh and blood children. I appreciate the closer concern of mothers and fathers. I simply want to put forward the importance for parents and all concerned in the development of young people of living honestly, prayerfully and openly, so that they may catch from you an integrity which speaks love, sympathy, solidarity and trust.

Marriage in the future

Not knowing where to start, I started on baptism, because that is where the individual begins. But the family in Catholic tradition starts from the giving and taking by two people of each other in marriage.

If it is important as I have stressed to get mother and father together to prepare for the baptism of their child, it is even more important to get a man and woman together to prepare for their married life. The importance of this is only highlighted by the difficulties. Most of us will know, from experience either as pastors, parents, relatives or friends, of 'shot-gun' marriages, of unions which we felt from the beginning were bound to fail, of apparently perfect combinations.

No matter what the situation may be, it is very strange that we have normally made so little of preparation for marriage.

Think that the whole life of two people is to be bound together till they die. What an enormously important action of mind, heart, faith, love and commitment! Add to this the dimension of children to accept, rear, educate and love; and again the social commitment of being married members of a community. Then realize that for many young couples there is little more to setting up their marriage than booking a hall for the reception, fixing the church, and concentrating on wedding accessories like music, flowers, cake, dresses, cars.

If, as I believe, family life is central and should remain central to Catholic Christian development in the 'family' world in which human beings live, then we must plan seriously to assist younger people to take their marriage preparation in mind, heart, love and commitment as more essential and more lastingly valuable than the trimmings. How can the Church (men and women, married and unmarried, clergy, sisters and every degree of life), assist the young

28

church (men, women, married, unmarried) to appreciate and accept the demands of commitment, the joy of commitment, and the lasting nature of commitment in the married life?

The witness of married couples

It is necessary—and I am very sorry there is any need—to make a clear and positive statement about married people. There are many, many couples who have made their commitment to each other in the presence of God, and who are faithfully living a growing, deepening, loving and witnessing married life together after five, eleven, fifteen, nineteen years of marriage and more. A very good number bear this witness in their lives with great happiness, and I know personally that it is lovely to be involved with joyous celebrations of silver, ruby, golden and diamond jubilees.

So often, everything seems depressing . . . everything seems to be falling apart, especially married life. The increase in the divorce rate horrifies some and leads others simply to accept it as a normal development in marital patterns. Instead of this, Christians should be joyfully showing to the doubting world that there is a fullness of challenge and love in encountering each other in marriage at a depth which encompasses sorrow, happiness and pain, patience and wholeness and which is lasting. This is not sad slavish upholding of church laws—it is full, happy love.

Here we should face openly the Catholic tradition of the unity and indissolubility of marriage. This still holds. But in the world of today, which sometimes has more honesty than the past, it is admitted that not every marriage blessed in church is either happy or fulfilled, and indeed some are not even valid, for various reasons. The development of psychology has opened up different aspects of consent, due discretion and so on. There is also clear evidence that marriages reach a stage of development or non-development when the breakdown between the two who have pledged themselves is total, and the question has to be asked and answered: Is this now a marriage in the Christian sense?

Some tentative, some radical steps have been taken in this discussion. There have been different results. The process of understanding in the Roman Catholic Church has meant that more grounds for declaring a marriage initially null have been agreed to by marriage tribunals. There has also been discussion about and in some cases agreement to the blessing of another marriage after a divorce, when no annulment has been granted.

The Synod of the Church of England has now agreed to the remarriage of divorced people on certain conditions, though the full conditions and legislation have still to be discussed and announced. In this discussion, it is seriously important to investigate the possibility of agreeing to grounds for nullity in the church sense, beyond the civil statement of divorce.

The opinion I would put forward for discussion if there is to be a new vision in the Church in regard to marriage is this.

It is good to see that the preamble to the Synod motion reads: 'Marriage should always be entered into as a lifelong commitment.' In order to make this intention on the part of the bride and bridegroom as clear and deep as is humanly possible, much more care must be taken in marriage preparation. Though there may have to be exceptions, it should be the general rule that a course of instruction lasting for weeks if not months should be held for both parties to the marriage. This should be the rule whether or not both parties are Christian, in order that they should have the chance to explore the future of marriage with a third party or parties, and incidentally probe deeper into their own commitment to each other, to marriage, and so on.

Here I am a bit out of my depth, because I am not clear about the rights of the Church of England as the Established Church, or the obligations which are incumbent on the Established Church. In the Roman Catholic Church we can make provisions about courses, number of instructions, commitment to permanency. Though no one enjoys doing so, it is possible to refuse to officiate for a couple if their dispositions are wrong from the angle of the Church's teaching. If any one may present him or herself for marriage before a priest of the Church of England as of right, this means that there is little possibility of setting up a stable procedure for verification of commitment.

Even with the Roman Catholic procedure, there are marriages which it is very difficult to 'feel' will work out in the long term, and yet it is even more difficult to head off the couple concerned. Once again, there would be a better outlook if the background within the family were loving, strong, tender and open to sharing the delights and problems of growing into marriage. But not everything is dependent upon the family. There is the wider community and there is the influence of the Church. This is no place for discussing Disestablishment. However, the issue needs to be kept to the front of any vision of renewal, with serious questions raised about what are arguably archaic constrictions on the mission of the Church of England so long as it remains the Established Church.

In England we have lost the extended family, except where it still clings among those who have more recently come from other continents. This has been more serious a loss than is generally admitted. The nuclear family is the poorer for the limitations on accommodation, the increase of old people's homes, the loss of accessible grannies and grandads. Children are especially vulnerable to this loss, and it is clear that the amount of person-hours that are no longer available to them can have a serious effect. Though there has grown up a sense that it is not good for the proverbial mother-in-law to be too much about with a newly married couple, there can be exaggeration of mother-in-law difficulties to the detriment of such family as extends beyond the nuclear pattern.

It is very difficult at this stage in our development to reopen the possibility of extended family living. Yet it should seriously be considered, if not under the same roof, at least in a looser local connection. This would mean the building up of local communities, so that older people were not isolated in homes filled with other old people, but were able to be more integrated into their own families and the neighbourhood. This is especially interesting as an idea when we look at the new trends in care for the terminally sick and dying. Whereas the hospice movement has been growing, and the wonderful experience of their caring way of life is making a deep impression, there is also growing the sense that large hospices are not really the answer. Instead the smaller hospice is coming in, and there is much effort to get as many terminally sick back into home care as possible. Of course, this is not always possible, but the ordinary family and the family of the Church should be thinking of the benefit to the invalid and the community though it costs in time, energy and caring.

As with so much, we come again to the question of priorities in life. Christ was constantly in a caring situation in his public life. The heart of Christianity must not be allowed to grow cold through institutionalization, and renewal of our hearts must take in the very real responsibility we have for the young and for the sick, handicapped and elderly. We have much to learn from them. They have so much to give us. I believe that any family can be the richer for having as part of it someone sick or handicapped. I realize that it costs. But the benefit for everyone is in deeper terms than the cost.

There will certainly be some who cannot cope with a sick husband or wife, if sick and elderly themselves; but probably more could cope, if there was a development of home-care services, and if parishes were able to bring some assistance to the aid of the less capable.

People speak a great deal of building community in neighbourhoods. The practical emergence of parochially sponsored efforts is still insignificant. Either people cannot be bothered, or the ideas are too new or there is real fear about what this may mean in terms of commitment.

Here starkly is the truth of the Christian dilemma. We learn to live at a certain standard. We have certain established values, accept only limited demands upon us. But when we come forward, as did the rich young man of the Gospel, we come forward because part of us is wanting to give more. And then we are faced with that young man's dilemma. . . . Yes, you can go on as you are. . . . *but* if you want to be perfect. . . , sell all, and follow me.

At this word, our selfish-self, feeling there is need for some safeguard which is sensible and right, fears invasion of privacy, invasion of our private time, demands beyond the reasonable.

I can only say that you should be of good heart at this point. You would not be human if you did not take a step back, hold your breath and begin to count your losses. In the jargon phrase, 'join the club'. We are all hit in the same way. But, if you can step forward a little, you will join another club which has stepped before you in the steps of the Master. You will find that this step has taken you into deeper hardship, greater demand, and powerlessness. But you will also find the burden light and sweet. Your growth will be a growth through pain and discouragement to joy.

The art of listening

God is the great listener. Out of his silent being, he is with us silently, he speaks to us silently, he asks us to learn the response which comes from the deep part of our being. He asks us to learn from him how to listen.

If we learn to listen to God, we can learn to listen to each other. Our selfish-self needs training and practice in the art of listening. The famous story of Martha and Mary in St Luke (Luke 10:38–42) gives a clue to our tendency to preoccupation at the simple level of analysis. Martha was busy with many things. So are we. The world, the worries, the cares flood in. Over against this, Mary sits there for the possibility of stopping, saying 'No' to demands, and making space for silence, listening and the chance to hear.

A modern version of the destructive nature of over-involvement with 'being busy about many things' is illustrated by the following excerpt from an American western local newspaper:

Dear Folks,
Thank you for everything, but I am going to Chicago to try to start some new kind of life. You asked me why I gave you so much trouble, and the answer is easy, but I am wondering if you will understand.

Remember when I was about six or seven and I wanted you just to listen to me? I remember all the nice things you gave me for Christmas and birthdays, and I was real happy with them for about a week. The rest of the year I really did not want presents. I just wanted you to listen to me like I was somebody who felt things too, because I remember when I was young I felt things. But you said you were too busy.

Mom, you are a wonderful cook, and you had everything so clean, and you were so tired doing all those things that made you busy. But you know, Mom, I would have liked bread and peanut butter just as well—if only you had sat down with me a little while during the day and said to me: 'Tell me all about it so I can maybe help you understand.'

And when Donna came, I couldn't understand why everyone made so much fuss, because I didn't think it was my fault that her hair is curly, and her teeth so white, and she doesn't have to wear glasses with thick lenses. Her school marks were better too.

If Donna ever has children, I hope you will tell her to pay some attention to the one who doesn't smile, because that one will really be crying inside. And when she is going to bake six dozen cakes, to make sure first that the kids don't want to tell her about a dream or a hope or something, because thoughts are important to small kids even though they don't have so many words to use when they tell about what they have inside them.

I think that kids who are tearing their hair about so many things that grown-ups are tearing *their* hair about, worrying, are really looking for someone with time to listen a few minutes, and who really would treat them as they would a grown up who would be useful to them. You know!—be polite to them. If you folks had ever said to me: 'Pardon', I'd have dropped dead! If anyone asks you where I am, tell them I've gone looking for someone with time, because I've got lots of things I want to talk about.

(Kansas City Star)

I wonder how many parents are deaf in this way to the cry of their children, because it has never entered their understanding of what it is to be, and to be a parent, that time, energy, love and generosity are ingredients which make up the real parents.

Sometimes our deafness is part of our make-up, and because no one has ever told us, we do not even know we are deaf. Sometimes it is due to our personal unwillingness to be committed to hearing, because what we hear may be unpleasant or demanding. If it is unwillingness, this may be a fear of truth, and an attempt to cover up gaps in our own personalities with activity and general busyness which leaves no time to reflect upon our weaknesses. Unfortunately, the filling up of gaps and holes prevents us from being available to others. In particular, we fear to enter the dark part of others, where lurk their fears, their secrets and their wounded selves. It is a natural reaction to shun these areas. But the Christian has a living part of his or her being which demands turning to and not turning away from, living alongside and not shunning. The Christian is to be a ready listener, a humble but generous co-operator, and a warm person who can lighten darkness and relieve fear, not by himself alone, but relying upon the power of God. The Christian

34

is not there always to 'jolly people along', but rather to weep sometimes, be silent sometimes and rejoice sometimes.

Like Christ, we are then offering the hospitality of ourselves to the need of the other, who is spiritually or emotionally naked, in prison, a stranger or sick. Hospitality is oneself. It is the centre of family and of all relationship.

Chapter 3

FRIENDS

You are my friends

St John's Gospel tells us that Jesus chose the tense and emotion-filled occasion of the Last Supper to speak to his followers of friendship and love. In my own life I have experienced moments of danger, approaching death, or even personal crisis, when relationship with another person quite suddenly deepens from mere acquaintance to friendship and to love. The followers of Jesus had such an experience that evening: 'This is my commandment, that you love one another as I have loved you. Greater love has no man than this, that a man lay down his life for his friends. You are my friends if you do what I command you' (John 15:12–14).

Scattered through the Old Testament are wonderful passages of the revelation of God's love and mercy. The covenant was established with Abraham (Gen. 17) for ever, and so Jeremiah could portray the Lord as saying: 'I have loved you with an everlasting love; therefore I have continued my faithfulness to you' (Jer. 31:3). Or Isaiah: 'As one whom his mother comforts, so I will comfort you' (Isa. 66:13).

Yet the message of love as preached and lived by Jesus Christ opens up, deepens and extends the whole concept of love. The treasure of the new covenant in his love fulfils the treasure of the old covenant. Growing in the friendship and love of Jesus, John sums up: 'God is love' (1 John 4:8).

Any other statement seems hollow when set alongside this simple direct assertion—God is love. How hard it is for human beings to accept such a statement in its simplicity! How easy it is to dispute the possibility of the statement being true! The soaring mystery of God, the glory of 'God is love', collides in the human mind and heart with evil, pain and even the mystery of death. Can God who is love be reconciled by the human mind with the destructive power of nature and of mankind?

Jesus Christ lives out his life on earth proclaiming the love of God for nature, for sparrows, but above all for human beings. He calls God 'Father' and tells us to do the same. He goes further than anyone else in demanding our response of love: 'But I say to you, Love your enemies and pray for those who persecute you, so that you may be sons of your Father who is in heaven; for he makes his sun rise on the evil and on the good, and sends rain on the just and on the unjust' (Matt. 5:44–5).

The joy radiating from Jesus' teaching is that he personally lives love. He chooses his friends and expresses friendship and love to them, but he also forgives and prays for his executioners. His love shows in his caring for the sick, in his love of all who are poor in any way, spiritually as well as materially.

From his example and teaching, his friends catch the seed of love which grows in them as they spread his teaching to all creation. But prior to that, after the experience of the Last Supper, they all fail Jesus who has been teaching them to love. Jesus himself continues to preach love through his suffering in the garden, on the way, and on the cross. The wonder of his love is that it does not fail, even when he is failed by his friends.

You and I are his friends. We fail him. He does not fail us . . . nor will he ever fail us. If we need reassurance we have only to look at how Jesus after his resurrection reaffirms Peter in his love. All his friends, apart from Judas who was the exception and not the rule, visibly persevered in his love and died in his love.

The fruit of this friendship and love was and is the fellowship and community of the Church, expressed in the individual members and the corporate caring which follow on Christ's words: 'Where two or three are gathered in my name, there am I in the midst of them' (Matt. 18:20). But it must always be remembered and emphasized that the Church is only as holy and as loving as its members are holy and loving, because Christ has left us as stewards: his friends, his co-workers, his witnesses.

It is imperative if we are to correspond to the loving message of Jesus Christ that each of us accepts fully both in mind and heart that we are truly loved by God, loved by Jesus. Though we are far removed from the original disciples in time, we are close in disci-

37

pleship. You are my friends! Our renewal begins on that note of confidence, a confidence offered by Jesus. We are not enemy, we are not servant, we are not distant acquaintance, we are friend. The prophet in the Old Testament spoke for God: 'I have loved you with an everlasting love' (Jer. 31:3). Jesus' friend John expressed the same knowledge and assurance of love and being loved when he wrote: 'In this is love, not that we loved God but that he loved us, and sent his Son to be the expiation for our sins' (1 John 4:10).

A modern Jewish writer put it in this way:

> The old joke tells about the astronauts.
> When they returned from outer space,
> a reporter asked the spacemen,
> 'Did you see God up there'?
> 'Yes, She is black.'
> So much for the old joke.
> But my God is no joke.
> My God is a friend
> And she is not a she.
> She is not a He either.
> He was made a He because
> it was He's
> that wrote the Bible!
> Those He's were male chauvinists.
> Which is as bad as being female chauvinists.
> He has no sex as we know it.
> It is a special category called
> Friend.
> It is people who move
> in mysterious ways.
> Therefore, MY FRIEND GOD
> must perform his wonders.
> My friend God minds his own business
> His business is US.
> And he listens to our troubles
> fifty-two billion hours a day.
> It's like Creation.
> God created the world in six days.
> BUT HOW LONG IS ONE OF GOD'S DAYS?

The relation of love and friendship

Sadly, love as expressed in Christ's message has been eroded in the twentieth century. The most damaging erosion has been in the value, the meaning, of the word 'love'. This word has been scattered round far and wide in literature, song, advertisement and TV, until it has become almost valueless. Part of what renewal implies is that we should renew our perception of love, for the Christian must not allow the general inflationary spiral to stand in the way of realizing the true dimension of the love of Jesus Christ, which is a target for us ordinary human beings in our seeking for our heart's desire— perfect love given and received.

The Catholic teaching is that each one of us is capable of loving, and each of us is lovable. This appreciation of human beings is heightened if we are able to give enough time and space to be still and silent with God, because this giving to him opens our hearts to the cost which relationship with him implies. He is friend. Friend Jesus speaks in terms of giving life for a friend. He did this for friend you and friend me. Once we have acknowledged that Jesus is friend, we know he will never lose us, however slack a friend we may be in return. But we do not necessarily live in that assurance.

Recently a friend of mine, a Methodist minister, had the tragic experience when he was driving his car of knocking down an old man who suddenly stepped off the curb in front of him. The old man died from his injuries, and my friend was utterly shaken, asking himself many questions about his worthiness to be a minister and to stand and preach to his people. But courageously he told his own congregation and others like ourselves, asking for our friendship and support in prayer. Eventually, when all the evidence was collected, he was declared to be completely blameless, but while we all waited in tension and suffering with him, we were all drawn together in love. And one day, when his door bell rang, he found outside a West Indian lady with her entire family. She told him he might not recognize her, because she did not often come to church, but he had once been round and prayed with her, so she decided she would come, in his moment of need, to bring her family to pray with him. She began to pray and roughly what she said was, 'God, I hope you are going to listen to me. You may not recognize me, or know my voice, because I don't often come to church or talk to you.

But I come to you because a friend of mine is in trouble, and I want you to help him . . .'.

I value this happening, because it points up for me the reality of trust and love which is in a person who is a friend of God, even distantly. Being truly human, the lady expresses the difficulty of keeping in touch with God, but she is boldly confident he has not cut her off and is still waiting to hear from her. She knows instinctively that his love is simple and everlasting. She has been touched by the Spirit of God's love, the Spirit who gives new vision, warms, and deepens the innermost nature of the individual. This is renewal. At any moment, the Spirit can set us on fire. When we know the love of God and accept his mercy, we are in a position to express that love to others in such a way that they may catch it and themselves be set on fire. And this is a whole dimension which is of vital importance today, because there are so many people who suffer guilt, or have a dark, sin-ridden sense, feeling cut off from love. They need the touch of the Spirit—the message of love and hope which is the message of Jesus, the Good News.

Of course there are many different meanings to the word love. Sadly, the word itself and the concept have been devalued by being over-used on the media. Love is quickly and too automatically featured as getting into bed together. This leads both to wrong ideas on sexuality and on love, and to real difficulty in forming ordinary friendship between boy and girl, man and woman.

Every human being is by nature gifted with sexuality. It is intimate and integral to our very being. Sexuality is there in everyone and has a fundamental part to play in all our human relationships, however distant and slender, however full and sexually complete. We are attracted to each other in many different ways; we are indifferent to each other in many different ways; and we are alienated from each other also in many different ways. Though we may not think so or recognize the fact, sexuality is always present even if only to a tiny degree. It is not a gift to be despised or feared, but to be rejoiced in and made part of our lives.

The relationship of one human being with another (whether this is husband—wife, parent—child, boy—girl, or relationship of the same sex) is fundamental to human society. Part of this relationship is the beautiful gift of God, sexuality. It is not of itself rude or crude, but sensitive, vital, delicate, warm, and almost overwhelmingly powerful. Perhaps because of its power, sexuality has often been kept secret and sacred, hidden from the eyes of children and indeed from their minds, tacitly banned from conversation, even given an evil image. Partly this is because we are afraid, but partly too because we have not reached the limits of knowledge about sexuality. Our danger is that when there is some mystery, some understanding beyond our immediate grasp, we can trivialize. And this I fear we do with sexuality in much public discussion, imagery and advertisement.

It is important that the Church should be thoroughly positive about sexuality, friendship and love. There has been quite an amount of writing and official statement from various denominations. Much of it has been good and fresh. It is sad when it does not penetrate to the mentality of the clergy or the people. Negative advice or admonition, especially to the young in these days leads to accentuating the very common idea that church-people are out of touch with reality. Then the young simply make up their own minds, prompted by the media. We in the Church are to blame if we allow the beauty, positive power and natural integral place of sexuality in human life to be falsely presented to the general public.

In this area, it is good if the nature of friendship and its development can be stressed. Friendship is a relationship which can begin very slowly over a period of acquaintance before it is realized; or it can happen quite suddenly from a crisis or a mutual realization of empathy—but of its nature it needs space to develop, time together, growing knowledge of each other. Knowledge can lead to interest, interest to further knowledge; interest can develop into affection, a closer and more open relationship, more sharing. There are lessons to be learnt in the art of listening, talking, receiving, giving. There is equality and inequality, the need to grow in patience, where some part of one personality jars with the other personality. Is difference to mean friction? Does growth lead to tolerance, understanding and acceptance of the other as he is or she is, not as I would like them to be?

Over a period of time, friendship can become binding, lasting even over long periods of separation. Friendship clearly is possible between those of different sexes or the same sex, younger and older, black and white, highly intelligent and the simple. There are endless permutations. There is always the fact that we are sexed beings,

41

but the important insight is that too much emphasis on the sexual fulfilment being essential and speedy for deep relationship can limit the possibility of friendship.

The Church has studied different and difficult sexual orientations. More study is needed. We are by no means clear yet about the whole of sexuality and especially we are not a hundred per cent clear on homosexuality. This is a live issue, because there are numbers, some say one in twenty, some say one in six, who maintain clearly that they are sexually orientated to their own sex. The character of homosexuality is, I believe, still not fully understood, and more study must be done. Also, there must be more listening to and understanding of the homosexual, in whatever walk of life he or she is. The sense of evil and nastiness which tends to pervade and dominate our mental reaction to homosexuality is hardly mature, and erupts in evil persecution. Where there is understanding, a readiness to listen and to accept the person for his or herself, the individual who is homosexual is able to be fully integrated in society; is a very valuable member of society, on a level with anyone else; and is free. Part of our personal and church renewal is in the acceptance of minorities and their rights. Where there are problems of conscience and morality unresolved, the Church has a duty to continue the search for justice, peace and love.

Jesus in his life managed to seek out the individual and in listening to each one, encouraging, reproving and building, helped people to become fully themselves, spiritually, physically, mentally and emotionally. He brings out in those he meets the basic qualities of relationship, the hard as well as the beautiful facets of love. St Paul sums up some of them: 'Love is patient and kind; love is not jealous or boastful; it is not arrogant or rude; . . . it does not rejoice at wrong, but rejoices in the right. Love bears all things, believes all things, hopes all things, endures all things. Love never ends' (1 Cor. 13:4–8).

The example of Mary
I want deliberately to insert here the example of Mary, Mother of the Lord. Her hospitality to the Spirit of God brings forth the Word of God, Jesus Christ, who is her son and our friend. This is possible by the power of the Spirit of God, because Mary is close to Jesus,

and open in her relationship and her life as we get glimpses of it in Scripture as the embodiment of Paul's words on love.

Both the Eastern Orthodox and the Catholic Church in the past have been redolent of devotion to Mary. It is not possible to go far in observing either Church without meeting Mary. 'The place accorded her in Catholic theology and devotion issues from the position she fills in the economy of revelation as the Mother of the Redeemer' (F. L. Cross, *Dictionary of the Christian Church*, 'Mary, the Blessed Virgin'). However, the intensity of medieval devotion led to the backlash of the Reformation period. This meant in practice that Marian devotion was ended in the Church of England, and indeed Mary became to a large extent a symbol of excesses in 'Roman' Catholicism. While this blindness grew to ignorance, the effect on the Church of Rome was if anything an intensification of interest by theologians, in between the Council of Trent and the nineteen-fifties. Titles of Mary were researched and new theories crystallized. At the same time the faithful centred much of their prayer life on the rosary and other devotions in honour of Our Lady. The main evening service on Sundays, and indeed weekdays as well, was some form of rosary, sermon and Benediction. Feasts of Our Lady scattered the liturgical calendar like stardust.

All of this development seemed to come to an abrupt halt when Vatican II opened the windows. A return to Scripture, the increase of Mass in the evening which cut out rosary, sermon and Benediction, and a compensation away from devotion to Mary on the part of many priests, were all strands which changed the spiritual climate. This was in a sense fostered by the fathers of Vatican II when they refused a separate document on Mary, and placed reference to her beautifully and centrally in the document on the Church: Mary, Mother of the Redeemer, is closely linked to the Church.

The temporary obscuring of Mary has cleared the air, and in the past decade new interest has begun to emerge. I believe myself that new vision in the life of the Church includes new vision of Mary, with a return to her relevance as Mother of Jesus. In order that this vision should be available in and beyond the Catholic Church, it is important that we should all be prepared to look at Mary afresh, to drop any traditional hostility or depreciation of her worth, and to see whether we can find place for her in our spiritual growth.

43

I am encouraged in this belief as I find both in the Church of England and in Methodism more openness to Mary, and the slow but steady growth of the use of the rosary, enjoyment of pilgrimages to Walsingham, Aylesford and Lourdes, and good work being done through the Ecumenical Society of the Blessed Virgin.

I put this section in friendship because of Mary's hospitality to the Spirit of God, which is an example to us of the inpouring of the Holy Spirit. In using Luke, I am not going into exegetical problems of the infancy narratives, but meditating on the text. And what comes out to me is the quality of receptivity in Mary. Though she seeks reassurance about the origin of the new vision presented to her, she then opens herself utterly: 'Behold, I am the handmaid of the Lord; let it be to me according to your word' (Luke 1:38). It is interesting that fear is also present, because this links with a very normal reaction in most of us when we allow God to enter our lives more deeply. We find it easier to rationalize, to pray on a cerebral level. The silence, the openness and the inability of our minds to grasp the height and depth may lead to a sense of helplessness, and even to panic.

But if we follow the example of Mary, then we shall be led along the path by the Spirit. In her case, the fullness of her availability, the fullness of her gift of self and the responding fullness of the gift of the Spirit, brought forth the Word of God.

We too in our response are given the opportunity by God for his spirit to be poured into our hearts, so that we bring forth Jesus to the world. 'Out of the abundance of the heart the mouth speaks' (Matt. 12:34).

Mary and others
Following the fullness of the Spirit within her, Mary went to see Elizabeth. I often think of this as the first charismatic prayer meeting: Elizabeth and Mary both filled with the Spirit, both shown to us as speaking from the heart, both recognizing in each other the wonderful works of God. But the visit is also typical of the friendship of Mary. Having listened to God, she heard; having heard, she went to her cousin. It is no surprise, then, that later in what sometimes has been interpreted as a 'brush-off' reference to Mary, Jesus says to the woman who raised her voice to declare blessed the womb

that bore him: 'Blessed rather are those who hear the word of God and keep it' (Luke 11:28).

There could be no more direct underlining of the quality of Mary's love and response than this. It sums up her life. It seals the three loves—God, herself, others. She does not thrust herself forward in the life of Christ. She is patient, she thinks of others, she lives out love of herself in bending to the will of God.

But, like each of us, she has to relate to her son, relate to people, relate to herself. When she loses Jesus in Jerusalem she is upset. When wine runs out at the wedding feast, she is concerned for the bridegroom. When she stands at the foot of the cross, she is in agony for her son.

We only catch a glimpse of Mary now and again, but each glimpse, if we seize it, teaches us intimately the reaction of the Spirit-filled human being to what is happening in life. We do not go through identical happenings, but we can relate what takes place in our lives to what happened to Jesus and Mary. We can learn to react out of the fullness of the Spirit, the fullness of the heart.

And so we find her eventually once more waiting upon and receiving the Spirit of God, in the upper room and at Pentecost. We might expect humanly that she would then be written up for all she did in spreading the gospel after Pentecost in the young Church. But no! Mary disappears. The openness, depth, intimacy and totality of giving which she expresses finds its fulfilment in silence.

Down the ages, there have been worries about saying something which either seems to elevate Mary to Jesus, to deify her; or seems to lower Jesus to be just another friend like Mary. If Mary was mother of Jesus, then there is no question but that she was special in that respect. No one else has ever borne Jesus and been so intimately connected as she was. But she is nevertheless one of us, and her close relation to Jesus in no way makes her divine.

I never really know how to get across the position of Mary in words which do not offend someone. So my resort is to the concept of the Communion of Saints, and strangely enough it can come across in the last of the mysteries of the rosary which has no biblical foundation, but sums up what I believe her position to be. The fifth Glorious Mystery is 'The crowning of Our Lady as Queen of Heaven and the glory of all the Saints'. She stands out from us, because God asked of her a special response. But from my viewpoint others stand out too—St John to whom Jesus entrusted Mary, St Paul, St Francis, St John Mary Vianney, St Thérèse of Lisieux. Then there are so many others in the many mansions promised by Jesus—Tertullian and Augustine, Cassian, the author of the Cloud of Unknowing, Luther, Thomas More, Dag Hammarskjöld, Padre Pio and my own mother and father. I cannot refuse a place with Jesus to his mother Mary: I read what she said and what she did responding to the will of God, and I am filled with admiration and a desire to do likewise. And then I turn to the whole throng of those who have gone ahead. Even the few I have known or know would fill more space than this whole book. I believe that in God's mercy, justice and love, they too are in heaven. If they are, they will rejoice among 'myriads of myriads and thousands of thousands, saying with a loud voice, "Worthy is the Lamb who was slain, to receive power and wealth and wisdom and might and honour and glory and blessing" ' (Rev. 5:11–12). Mary, Mother of Jesus, will, as it were, be leading the chorus . . . hopefully in death we shall all be there too! Meanwhile, there is plenty of room for us to honour Mary, to honour the saints, to try to learn from their example, and yet always to know that Jesus is Lord, Jesus is Redeemer, Jesus is friend differently from all our other friends in heaven.

Chapter 4

RECONCILIATION

He came to preach peace

There is a beautiful passage in the Letter to the Church at Ephesus:
'For he is our peace, who has made us both one, and has broken
down the dividing wall of hostility, by abolishing in his flesh the
law of commandments and ordinances, that he might create in
himself one new man in place of the two, so making peace, and
might reconcile us both to God in one body through the cross,
thereby bringing the hostility to an end. And he came and preached
peace to you who were far off and peace to those who were near;
for through him we both have access in one Spirit to the Father'
(Eph. 2:14–18).

Reconciliation is central to the work of Christ in this world—a
reconciliation which brings together opposition, discovers a path
through paradox, and essentially is a healing process. Because this
is his work, it must be our work also. We too must find our way
through paradox, and be reconciled and reconcile.

Reconciliation as a theme is older than the incarnation. Jesus
takes up the Old Testament theme in his life and teaching. The
Catholic teaching on reconciliation has taken its origin from and
closely adhered to the biblical revelation of sin and redemption.
The shrouded mystery of the beginning, the sense of mess and
dislocation and imperfection have all been referred back to a 'prim-
eval calamity', from which emerges the state in which we find
ourselves living. Against this some will rebel with a sense of injustice
done because we are not responsible. But anyway here we are! And
men and women living both before and since Christ have been
individually and collectively caught up in personal imperfection and
outright evil.

God's message to the world involved in this mess was to send his

Son, born into the world as a child, and from that moment undergoing the life of the human being. At one level, we can then watch what the mess of the world does to him, mainly through the tangle of human emotions—pride, anger, self-righteousness and so on. Some of this seems so general that it can only be expected from the state of the world and society—religious rivalry, political intrigue and poverty for instance. This is only sin in a very wide sense, yet in the life of Christ and afterwards of his followers, there emerges a 'social dimension' of sin and reconciliation, to which reference will be made later.

Meanwhile Jesus, who lives through the situation, begins to counter the live, actual faults and failings as he meets them in individuals and groups. He pins down hypocrisy, pride, disbelief, greed and sexual immorality when he meets them—actual human beings entering into actual human acts which are contrary to the law of God, the three loves of self, neighbour and God.

So, if we read and study the life of Jesus, we shall be blind if we do not see that to him sin is very real. He goes about healing physically and mentally, but always includes the spiritual—'Sin no more!'; and the positive contrast to disbelief—'Your faith has saved you.' He is warning against temptation to sin, and his whole attitude and way of living and meeting people is an exposition of his certainty of the merciful love of God who reconciles even the hardened sinner and gives hope where before there was none. But notice that, as St Paul points out, he has broken down the dividing wall of hostility and he is abolishing in his flesh the law of commandments and ordinances, that he might . . . reconcile us both to God.

If you and I are to enter into reconciliation, we have to accept the same condition . . . it is to be worked out in and through us. We cannot be detached; we must be involved. It will not be painless but painful. But for this involvement, it is necessary that we have a close relationship to Jesus through our prayer and contemplation because the world, of which we are part, is largely losing touch with God, has lost a sense of personal sin and has rejected any wide involvement in the turmoil with which we are faced in the world today.

What is sin? If it is a breakdown in relationship with God, it cannot consciously exist if you do not believe in God. But if you do believe in God it can be a very real reality. Jesus goes out into the desert to face the reality of Evil, however precisely we understand 'Satan', the 'Devil'. Today this reality is often pooh-poohed. For the Christian of the Catholic tradition Evil exists, and so we must also face this Evil. The din and tumult of business in the world can cover its existence and obscure our vision of it. Therefore with Jesus we need our own desert experience. It is made up of our will making a space for God in our lives, together with our facing out the fear that will come when we are alone and silent and all that is unpleasant or terrifying within us wells up and threatens to knock us off balance.

But harking back to the first chapter, we are to face up and not run away. True facing up acknowledges failure and sin in ourselves, as well as the healing power of God. Running away is nonsense; we cannot hide from God:

> Whither shall I go from thy Spirit?
> Or whither shall I flee from thy presence?
> If I ascend to heaven, thou art there!
> If I make my bed in Sheol, thou art there!
> If I take the wings of the morning
>   and dwell in the uttermost parts of the sea,
> even there thy hand shall lead me,
> and thy right hand shall hold me.
>
> (Psalm 139:7–10)

With Christ, it is for us to face sin in ourselves as well as evil in the world, but to realize reconciliation, redemption, in him:

> For in him all the fullness of God was pleased to dwell,
> and through him to reconcile to himself all things,
> whether on earth or in heaven,
> making peace by the blood of his cross.
>
> (Col. 1:19–20)

Jesus Christ's whole life, passion and death shout out to us the way we are being called to follow; and his resurrection binds together life here and hereafter, assuring us of the accomplishment of reconciliation, driving out of us hopelessness or despair.

The Ministry of Reconciliation

There is a long and tortuous history to the Church's interpretation of forgiveness of sin. The Catholic tradition taught by the Church of Rome has varied the frequency, purpose and structure of the sacrament of penance or reconciliation. In the beginning it was for use once in a lifetime, then it became more frequent, and even excessively frequent and rather a routine. Just recently, there has been some rethinking and redirection; confession is now often less frequent but more open and more linked to spiritual guidance as well as the forgiveness of sin.

In the Church of England, there has always been provision for a penitent to come to a minister, to confess sin, and to receive guidance and an assurance of God's forgiveness. But the use of such a ministry has been patchy, and it is probably true that a large number of people have never practised confession and would not readily see the purpose of it.

As part of the new way of life which is seen as the purpose behind Catholic Renewal, the rediscovery of the ministry of reconciliation is very important. It may seem odd for me to stress that at a time when the practice has, to some extent, faded among Roman Catholics, but this fading is partly an adjustment away from what I would term the weekly-quick-in-quick-out confession, and a move towards a wider and deeper examination of life.

Briefly, the purpose of my submitting myself to the minister of the Church and doing so through the ministry of another human being is to make a public expression of my sorrow. It is public because it is through the priest, not because it is done with lots of other people listening. It is an act of humility wherein I accept the authority of the Church as guardian and guide to the holy things of God. I accept my fellow human being as someone better able than myself to make a judgment of where I stand, of my guilt—and of my goodness; and I accept through his word the promised forgiveness of God, who knows me through and through. This practice brings peace of mind and soul, a deeper trust in God, and a facing of the reality of sin in my life as something to be tackled in the future, once it is clear that the past is no more a burden, that guilt does not remain, that there is nothing to hold me back.

Confession to another person is no running away, no covering up of sinfulness. Though secrecy is enjoined upon the priest, it is a secrecy which he finds easy to maintain, a secrecy that is not 'shy-making' when the penitent is later met in a public setting. For the priest it is a continuous sense of joy and admiration at the humility, courage, perseverance and good lives of so many ordinary people, normally unrecognized. For the penitent, it is often an immense relief to have verbalized a failure, to have shared a painful episode of which he is not proud, to have been assured that he has come to the merciful love of God and that forgiveness is there.

Traditionally, spiritual direction has gone hand in hand with the practice of confession. The priest is a doctor for the soul. He is not only there to distinguish the disease in a person but to suggest treatment, to bring the person nearer the will of God, nearer perfection. So, in sharing a burden, in trusting another with our intimate state of soul, we can hope also for a pointer towards the future. This supposes we have found a wise spiritual counsellor. We are meant to be on the way to God's Kingdom. If there is no guide it is very easy to get lost up a cul-de-sac or simply to stop trying to go anywhere.

But bringing myself to confession and asking for guidance implies that I accept I am a sinner, that I need reconciliation, and that I value the ministry of the Church. If this ministry is to be useful, it implies the co-operation of mankind with God. In other words, priests must be properly trained; and human training is not enough. Good guides grow through training, but also through prayer and a deepening spiritual life, together with an interest in people and a desire to help. They are not counsellors in a professional or psychiatric sense . . . they are priests. The foundation training is knowledge and love of God, living a life of the following of Jesus Christ, and holiness. Sin and holiness essentially have to do with relationship to God and not with medical psychology; spiritual guidance should have the same origin.

Digression on the Vertical
However, there must be a note of warning. The purpose of the sacrament and ministry of reconciliation, examination of conscience, and forgiveness is not to make each person thoroughly introspective.

When I undertook to try to write something for the Catholic Renewal Movement in the Church of England, I spent about a year looking and listening. I heard many things, good, mediocre and bad, as you might expect. But one line repeated itself with considerable frequency, and it has its place here. Look at it, listen to it, and do not necessarily dismiss it out of hand. A number of people honestly think it is true. The line was one of criticism. The movement, it went, is inclined to be inward-looking. People are so concerned with their own development and holiness, they are rather detached from the real world. They are a small body of people, self-concerned, busy with liturgical things, and, as one person put it very disparagingly, with self-titillation.

This leads me to insert here a distinction which was used a lot in the recent past . . . the difference between the horizontal and the vertical approach to God. The horizontalists maintained strongly the immanence of God in the world and especially in mankind: the way to meet God was through and in the world, meeting other people; there was nothing to be gained by removal of oneself to pray alone. The verticalists asserted that deep, personal prayer and the whole development of the spiritual life towards God were the direct way of meeting and coming to know and love God. To me, both of these approaches are valid, but both have dangers.

The danger with the vertical approach is that it is possible so to concentrate upon discipline and the singular importance of the direct relationship with God that the individual isolates himself from the world and its problems: the triangle of the three loves becomes unbalanced—God and self predominate over love and care for the neighbour. The result is narcissism.

This is the criticism which lies behind those who have spoken to me unfavourably about the Renewal Movement in the Church of England. To some degree, the criticism is valid, and to some degree it is also valid for other renewal movements in other denominations.

However, though there is danger here, it is not an inevitable feature. Let me give you an example from St Thérèse of Lisieux. This very Catholic young woman was always conscious of Jesus as reconciler. Through her contemplation she came to realize that the torn and bloodied face of Christ as so often seen in art, particularly for many on the Shroud of Turin, was the expression of the merciful love of God. For her this was the cost of that love which makes man one again with God in Jesus' mysterious act of self-giving. 'For it is the God who said, "Let light shine out of darkness," who has shone in our hearts to give the light of the knowledge of the glory of God in the face of Christ' (2 Cor. 4:6), who now risen from the dead stands to intercede for us. That merciful love, she realized, is closely involved with people of the world since Christ the priest 'always lives to make intercession for them' (Heb. 7:25). As she grew, Thérèse became not more and more introverted, but ever more aware of the reality which had made her anxious in her young days for the soul of a notorious murderer, Pranzini. She herself prayed secretly for him and later for many others, especially for missionaries in distant lands, for whom she offered her prayer and her physical and spiritual suffering. This vertically living nun, in an enclosed convent, was later accepted as a beacon for very ordinary people in the world and as a patron for all missionaries by the Roman Catholic Church.

I personally, from the moment of God rediscovering me in disbelief, have been a verticalist, but always with the very clear notion that the giving of space and time to God in prayer as a first essential to spiritual living, leads surely and inevitably to action in God's world for God's people.

Action may not necessarily be the right word. In reality, what I am saying is that if you spend time with God deeply and in stillness, you will become aware of evil and sin, in yourself and the world; you will be sensitive to injustice at home and abroad; you will feel a solidarity with the oppressed. Just how far such solidarity is expressed in action or how far it is solidarity in mind, heart and prayer has to be sorted out in each particular person's life. What is quite clear is that God is not cut off from the predicament of the world, and so no true development within the Church can afford to be introspective, cliquish or narcissistic.

Jesus Christ the path-finder through paradox, lived years in silence, inactivity and hiddenness. Later he combined long periods of prayer with intense activity. What an example. . . and how can we combine the two? It is no wonder that we find it hard to reconcile the apparently irreconcilable, and so edit the life of Christ to our seemingly lower capability.

The social aspect of reconciliation

To some extent in the past, the very form of the sacrament of penance or reconciliation within the Roman Catholic Church emphasized the vertical. The privacy of the confessional, the relationship of the penitent to God, the sense of personal guilt, the desire to realize one's own personal release from sin—all this led to introspection and keeping an eye on personal sanctification.

In the much older order, which has now been revived in modern thinking and practice, sin was not only personal, but very much a community affair. The public ejection of a member from the worship of the community, and the subsequent public readmission was strongly communal. Both the Eucharist and reconciliation traditionally are community acts, which highlight the good of worshipping together, and the harm which reacts upon the public by the ungodly and unsocial act of an individual or a group.

The strong line of thinking and teaching today about the immanence of God in his creation is an added reason for us to adopt in any attitude to the ministry of reconciliation this more social aspect. Especially for many young people, for whom distinctions between right and wrong in personal life are somewhat blurred (and for whom the notion of sin is more in relation to the evils in society than in direct relation to the transcendent God), an examination of conscience in terms of justice, peace, poverty and so on is more immediate and more personally challenging.

If there is danger for the verticalist in becoming too introverted, there is the opposing danger for the horizontalist in becoming too extroverted. The needs of society cry out to us and remind us that Christ came to give the good news to the poor. We have a responsibility to do the same, and to live in relation to them and to strive for justice and peace.

To get involved in the betterment of the world is good, indeed essential, but it must not be to the exclusion of the God dimension. From personal experience I have sometimes felt the weight of a certain problem lying on my own shoulders, with the whole resolution depending upon the insight and temporal muscle of a particular party or philosophy, without recourse to prayer.

The balance of horizontal and vertical in life becomes more crucial as we face extraordinary economic readjustment, political forces gathering strongly to right and left in opposing policies, and at the same time a certain pull among some church-people to run for the desert. Renewal must face the situaton as it is, and by analysing it prayerfully and rationally use the intelligence which God has given us, while at the same time relying upon the wisdom and guidance of the Spirit.

An examination of conscience

The ministry of reconciliation has been known as the sacrament of pardon and peace. In laying ourselves open to Christ, we can look at ourselves not in isolation but in the light of his words and his example when he lived in this world. For anyone who uses the ministry of reconciliation there is an opportunity to meet Christ in a very special way, a way we can recognize from the numerous meetings that Jesus himself had with individuals whose healing he undertook, from sickness and from sin. We face judgement from him here and now, as we believe we will one day face him when we die. Now the first question is simply: Do you love me?, a question touching my direct and personal response to his love in the deepening of prayer, worship and the seeking of God's will, his love. The second question is: When I was hungry, thirsty, naked, in prison, did you . . .?, a question touching the here and now of my life in this world, in relation to himself, immanent in people and nature.

Take the longish passage in 1 John 3:3–24 as a basis for examination. It would be as well to read it through first of all, but I only draw on certain lines.

John writes of living a holy life when he says: 'He who does right is righteous, as he is righteous' (3.7). For some people righteousness is centred entirely on their relation to God; so long as they feel right with God, they are able to isolate themselves from neighbourhood problems and the sufferings of the world. The stress on righteousness certainly faces us with God, the first love, whom we are to love with our whole being. This reflects back onto myself, who am loved by God. But John immediately in this passage faces us with the third aspect of love, and makes its inclusion an imperative:

> By this it may be seen who are the children of God, and who are the children of the devil: whoever does not do right is not of God, nor he who does not love his brother (v.10).

55

And later on he underlines his point:

By this we know love, that he laid down his life for us; and we ought to lay down our lives for the brethren (v.16).

Thus, the Christian has a responsibility which is not simply vertical, but very definitely horizontal and extroverted. It is in this regard that we must consider ourselves, our righteousness, our holy life as lived in the world, and responsible to and for the world. This has been true in history, whether recognized or not, and it is true today.

The thrust and development of our Christian society in western Europe and its outreach have been behind the political, social, economic and scientific development of the past centuries which is largely responsible for the world situation of today. It is not my intention to wallow in guilt and breast-beating. But it is important when we are engaged in what we hope will be a new vision for us in the life of the Church that we should be aware both of how we have led the world and been led by the world in the past. Our mandate as followers of Jesus Christ is to go out, not to stay within the closed community of our church porch and the limited number who worship with us.

Looking round we can make lists of whole areas of life which should draw the attention and compassion of anyone who claims to be studying the message of Jesus Christ and trying to live out his call. Not only are large sections of society 'out of touch' with God, but political and economic power seems largely to favour the already favoured, at the expense of the already oppressed.

There have been some fine efforts to rethink the word of Christ to the world in terms which are liberating and powerful. But all too often the Church is seen to be on the side of the 'haves', not the 'have-nots'; and when elements of the Church appear on the side of the oppressed, they tend to be picked off by the establisment as being political and being out of step with orthodoxy.

It is here that a serious examination of conscience is necessary. So much of what has been good in the Catholic movement in the Church of England in the past century has been involvement with the poor in the cities, the living alongside stress and deprivation in slums and the wasteland. To live out the incarnation is to be in the midst of the world as it is, especially in those inner city areas from which others, even in the caring professions, are now withdrawing from actually living among those they serve.

By allowing the values of society to lean heavily on money earned, on the right to a steady annual increase in the standard of living, on annual pay rises, we Christians have accepted a standard which is totally materialistic. Happiness is valued by money. The real values of family love, sharing, seeking the good of others as well as personal enrichment—these are lost. But we have gone along with the economic development of our country, which has included exploitation in our own society, in other countries and of the world's resources. Against such abuses, there have been protests, but weak ones.

If there is to be Catholic renewal which has impact, it will mean not only a verbal warning to society but a forceful and—it is to be hoped—concerted effort by the Christian churches (and that means chiefly by those individuals who subscribe to church membership) to change their material expectations and necessarily their life-style. This is not at all to say out of hand that progress and development towards better standards of living are wrong. But it is to get a balance in priorities so that we remember that God is central to our living, that the material is passing, and that our true happiness will derive from an integration of the material and the spiritual—such that we are neither deprived of the spiritual by the material nor deprived of the material by the spiritual.

God is the God of all human beings. He has no brief for an exclusive clique. He works for the salvation of all. This is implied in the passage from 1 John. Others outside our small circle are included. We must look out for the other. God is not impotent, nor does world development cut him off from his creation. But can we see any way in which thoughtful action could lead the world to rethink attitudes and policies?

It is easy to talk in terms of a change of life-style. But what would that mean personally, and how would it be effective? There are so many levels of living, it is both hard and also probably absurd to try to make suggestions. Once again, you will be better aware of possibilities if you pray deeply, and are prepared to share some of your thoughts, feelings and insights with others. It may mean rethinking food or fuel consumption, the use of cars, pollution, an attitude to nuclear disarmament including unilateral, the possibility of sharing various facilities with others, conservation and ecology, the work in the world which we and our successors should be doing.

At any time in history, the current generations are involved in living by tilling the soil, fishing, manufacturing, administration, doing educational, clerical and manual work. Others have the task of defending the community, doing research work, caring for the needs of the poor, the sick, aged and many others through medical and social work. If we are doing this for God, and not just for our own ends, gratification and enrichment, then we can listen to St Paul: 'I appeal to you therefore, brethren, by the mercies of God, to present your bodies as a living sacrifice, holy and acceptable to God, which is your spiritual worship. Do not be conformed to this world but be transformed by the renewal of your mind, that you may prove what is the will of God, what is good and acceptable and perfect' (Rom. 12:1–2).

Of Jesus we read at the beginning of this chapter how he broke down the barriers, destroying in his own body the hostility. This is our function too, if we can find how we can change our whole way of life and life-style. It is clear that there is a vacuum in society which is being filled with completely materialistic expectations— hopes and goals beyond our scope. Yet it is not a strong society. It is fragile without the Christian perspective of the equal rights of all mankind, it can collapse in violence. Where do we stand?

If we truly believe, we should follow Jesus Christ, the poor man of Nazareth. Can we truly say we are in fact doing so, setting an example? It is put quite starkly by St John: 'But if anyone has the world's goods and sees his brother in need, yet closes his heart against him, how does God's love abide in him?' (1 John 3:17).

And really, in the situation in which we now are, Catholic, Christian, non-christian—Church and state alike—it is very difficult to see that we are responding to John's teaching: 'Little children, let us not love in word or speech but in deed and in truth. By this we shall know that we are of the truth, and reassure our hearts before him whenever our hearts condemn us; for God is greater than our hearts, and he knows everything' (vv. 18–20).

Frankly, we are caught in this society. But Jesus went about living and teaching in such a way that he raised opposition, and it was thus in his own person he killed the hostility—by being killed himself. Is there no way in which renewal can and should face this challenge? Is the Church as institution herself compounding the injustice by continually finding more reasons to raise money, and continuing to live beyond the means of the poor?

Is she aligned with the rich and the established, and so afraid to advocate radical reappraisal of resources? Is she in danger of being hypocritical? Is her doctrine based upon a theology which states, as a senior cleric is recently reported to have stated, that money is as real as the Holy Trinity?

It is easy to ask such questions of 'the Church'. When it comes down to it, we are the Church at all levels. Are we not ourselves compounding the folly of the world by refusing to listen to the folly of Christ? I do not believe that we can honestly witness to Christ on the street, in the countryside, on the paddy field or anywhere in the world unless we take seriously the call of St Paul: 'Put off your old nature which belongs to your former manner of life and is corrupt through deceitful lusts, and be renewed in the spirit of your minds, and put on the new nature, created after the likeness of God in true righteousness and holiness (Eph. 4:22–4).

I do not set out here to give you a programme which will involve supporting this action or doing that action, giving up this and taking on that. In a thoroughly practical way, the message is one of attitude, change of mind, change of heart as preached by the prophet Joel: 'Return to me with all your heart, with fasting, with weeping, and with mourning; and rend your hearts and not your garments' (Joel 2:12–13).

It is difficult for me to be at peace with my conscience when I am involved in so much ordinary living and acceptance which seems opposed to Christ's call. Yet I do go on, I do compromise, I do live more richly than I should; and I am slow to say the unpopular thing, to take a stand against waste, and so on. It is a really deep temptation to reconcile Christian teaching to the status quo in Church and state—but this is not the reconciliation which this chapter is speaking about. I am condemned by my own admissions; but, in saying that, I am determined to go away and read James 4:13—5:6 and Mark 10:17–22. Will you do the same, and have a pondering session, before you begin the next chapter?

59

Chapter 5

THE LOCAL CHURCH

What is the local church?

It used to be comparatively simple to know the local church as regards both towns and villages. Probably most people knew the vicar, priest or minister, or all three if there were three! This can still remain true today, though amalgamation of parishes, widening of circuits and so on often make the local clerical leader a more diffused person. In great urban complexes and in cities, the crowding and overlapping, the mobility and commuting, the weekday and weekend allegiance all help to create a very different atmosphere to 'parochial belonging'.

In the inner city, boundaries are practically meaningless, but sometimes still clung to by clergy and parochial church councils. In London, a number of churches I know in the inner city are to all intents and purposes kept going by a faithful few who commute in still for Sunday worship. Other churches accepting the weekend desert make themselves a weekday centre of worship, instruction and entertainment, with considerable support schemes to tackle local needs in homelessness, vagrancy, alcoholism, drug addiction or prostitution.

Efforts have been made with team ministries and other permutations. People are still finding their way to suitable life-styles and methods of sharing, teaming, working individually and together. Happily much of this is now thought of in ecumenical terms as it should be.

To my mind, the local church in the city must strive to have good relationship in every direction with other churches, communities and organizations which are in and of the area, and have as the purpose of its presence the care, support and upbuilding of the locality, whether the latter is seen in religious terms or simply in community terms. Inner city breakdown is a phenomenon of our time. Different efforts have been made but the inner city seems to remain an intractable situation. Here neighbourhood unity is difficult, housing often poor to horrifying; families find living difficult in high-rise flats or grotty older buildings; police relations vary from excellent community policing to occasions of disastrous breakdown, leading to distrust and issuing in violence. The possibilities for the immediate future in the inner cities could be dire and horrendous. It will take combined effort, love, care, wisdom, and a hundred and one other virtues to prevent a total collapse. It will take even more in vision, co-operation, leadership and charisma to build something which is just, peaceful and authentic.

This being said, I am full of hope and excitement because the inner city is in a uniquely strong position, provided that it is seen by those in authority to be important and is staffed with handpicked personnel. These persons should be people of prayer, who rely upon God utterly, and who are prepared to suffer and enjoy the hardship, deprivations, violence and other elements which will be part of the local atmosphere, and which are to be harnessed to developing the future. Here the Church has a wonderful opportunity for pathfinding and paradox reconciliation, if only there is courage at all levels to seize the now.

How this will apply in more rural and open areas, I cannot say, because I do not have the experience; but so far as my observation has gone there is a greater conservatism of approach in the more country and suburban districts, which will need a deal of nurturing, leading and prophetic ministry if congregations are going to be opened to the movement of the Spirit towards a new vision of the life of the Church in today's world.

The place of the Eucharist

In Catholic teaching, the Church is centred on the Eucharist. Any new vision of the life and work of the Church, if it is to be Catholic, must have this central emphasis on the Eucharist. There is no substitute, there is no alternative. 'Take, eat; this is my body' (Matt. 26:26). 'Do this in remembrance of me' (Luke 22:19). The witness of the early Church is that they did this (Acts 2:42), and the tradition is marked by St Paul (1 Cor. 11:23–9).

Because this is so close to the living heart of Christianity it is a sensitive area. Jealously guarded, it has sadly become the centre of dispute, when it was instituted as the centre of love. But just because it is so central in the living of Christianity, we must be doubly sure that the Mass, the Eucharist, is alive in the minds, hearts and worship of all who are committed to the new life in Christ, to Catholic Renewal.

Our belief is the foundation from which we worship. If we do not believe in God, we shall not worship God. If we do believe, then as Christians we believe not only in God, but in the one he sent, his Son, known to us as Jesus Christ. All prayer in worship is through Jesus Christ for he is Son of God, and our Redeemer. This is Catholic faith.

The general pattern of the Mass grew from the inheritance of the ways of worship in the Old Testament with the use of prayers, psalms and readings, which at first were probably still based within the synagogue setting, and gradually were attached to the more separate worship of the breaking of bread.

This is no place for an exposition of the history of the Eucharist. It has been through many changes of form, but the Catholic teaching is that from the early days until the present time, the central purpose and action has remained the re-enactment of the Last Supper, of Jesus' life, death and resurrection, presided over by an ordained minister.

What is important for the local Church is that there should be good, strong and clear teaching for all the congregation about the depth and meaning of the Eucharist; and that it should be by conviction as well as by devotion a magnet drawing the local community together in prayer and praise to hear the word of God, to share in the sacrifice and sacrament. For the priest, then, the Mass in one sense is his central action of the day. Through the Mass he is to gather the people of his community, young and old alike, to form Eucharist by their gathering. He is to instruct them in the personal and community aspects of the liturgy. He is responsible for their realizing that they come together humbly as sinners to acknowledge the healing and forgiveness of Jesus in their lives. Moreover, he is there not only to read the word of God so that they can listen and hear, but also to expound that word.

This latter duty places on the shoulders of the priest the mantle of the preacher and even the prophet. It should mean that he must be earnest both in his study of Scripture and in his deep and prolonged periods of daily prayer. He is not speaking for himself, but speaking the word of God. He is not speaking to himself, he is speaking to the people of God. He therefore has the additional call to know the people, to penetrate their need (material and spiritual), to speak from where they are and lead them to a greater knowledge and love of God. Not only does his personal commitment and spirituality show through as he speaks, but perhaps even more clearly it is reflected by the manner in which he celebrates the mystery of the Mass.

One of the points of renewal for both priest and people is the recognition and living out of the holiness of the Mass, to which each person comes to share with others whatever he or she has brought in personal commitment. Though the Mass is the work of God, he has left us to bring it into being by our presence and our participation. Today, this has been emphasized in a clearer way by various changes which have taken place, though not all of these have filtered through to all parishes.

To a large extent in the older church liturgies, the celebration of the Mass was simply a priestly activity. Nowadays the division of ministries has become more plain. With the sharing of readings, a fuller part in the prayers at Mass, a greater emphasis on the singing of the congregation rather than the choir, with stress on the reception of holy communion as an integral part of the Mass, and lay participation in the distribution of holy communion—in all these ways the community nature of worship has been opened up. Though there has still not been enough thought or writing about the priesthood of the people, there is the glimmering of a new understanding, even within the jealously guarded limits of the Mass, of the exclamation of St Peter: 'But you are a chosen race, a royal priesthood, a holy nation, God's own people, that you may declare the wonderful deeds of him who called you out of darkness into his marvellous light. Once you were no people but now you are God's people; once you had not received mercy but now you have received mercy' (1 Peter 2:9–10).

The Eucharist and the People of God

The changes which have taken place in the form of service in most Christian churches in recent years are significant. In Eastern Orthodox churches, there has been little change. Among most of those which have an original Roman or European base after Jerusalem, and may be called western, there has been a coming closer both of language and layout, so that a stranger attending the Eucharist service in the Church of England, Roman Catholic or even Methodist Church might be confused as to which denomination he was worshipping with.

Those who dislike the movement tend to say that in all this there has been a paring down and adaptation which has so mutilated the beauty of the older forms that the new words, forms and even content appear empty, flat and lifeless.

The churches however maintain that there is continuity, and it would seem that, with this assured, the onus now lies on priest and people to grow into the new forms so that the community itself enlivens them in the ways which are open. If the new forms are used in exactly the same very priestly way that the old forms were, the likelihood is that there will be little beauty in the liturgy. This is because the thrust of the reforms is towards what in the media would be called 'audience participation'. The Mass was always meant to be alive with audience participation, but it gradually became removed from the people. Now it is back among the people, and some people don't like it coming back, while others don't know what to do with it; they are dismayed at being so close, and 'losing the mystery'.

Rather than lamenting the past, renewal should take hold of what is presented and study how best this new form can be used for the worship of God through the prayer and praise of priest and people. In the first place this puts a demand upon the clergy. But think now of the part of the people. How can each person become a more worshipping sharer in the Mass?

Speaking as a Roman Catholic, I am convinced that the new liturgy has not succeeded as well as it should have done because it was not sufficiently preached, explained and discussed. It happened piecemeal, often with the grudging acceptance of the clergy. God has given us intelligence, which he expects us to use for ourselves and others in his service. Especially in the audio-visual world of today, there is much less blind acceptance; much more questioning and desire to 'be in on the act'. Wherever we are we must seize this opportunity for opening up the riches of the Mass, explaining and discussing change and the reason for it, so that we can *all* be involved more fully.

The older rites and times were very formal when looked at from our present climate of informality and greater openness. Sunday was a day to dress up for church-going; having nothing good enough to wear was a reason not to attend. People were cut off from the priest, and did not expect to participate very much in the ceremony, unless they were of the small group which formed choir, servers or sidesmen. Among Anglicans in England this was more true than among Roman Catholics. Though I can personally remember back to elaborate ceremonies at the altar, while the congregation was silent and stiff in the pews, there was with us always the likelihood of crying children (who indeed got 'tutted' at by the pious), and some people came late and left early. Since Vatican II, the whole atmosphere has changed, except in churches where the priest finds change difficult. On the whole, the feeling generated by the change has been one of welcoming, friendliness and a greater openness in ceremonial, sharing and interest.

The important stress at this point for those who are afraid of change or feel horror at the greater freedom of expression is that these innovations do not spell the end of ceremonial and ritual, but present them from a new angle. After all, when numbers are involved in any meeting or assembly, the conduct of the 'platform' and the 'auditorium' can vary from preaching to a captive audience to sharing in dialogue and discussion. But the preparation of the 'meeting' can also be shared.

One of the ways of assisting in this is with the training of readers, servers, choir, and others, not only in reading or serving or singing but in greater and more prayerful sharing in the whole essence of eucharistic worship. And it should not be the priest who is doing this all the time. He can train other trainers and so spread the knowledge and the sense of participation.

There are today many excellent courses, day, weekend or even longer, which are geared towards this sharing. Often new insights can be gained by attending such a course which is not of your own churchmanship. Any living local church should be living not just parochially but also from the knowledge and strength of the wider Church.

Today there is a broader sharing of the ministry of the word, and I hope a greater emphasis on the importance of the Eucharist in worship. Where church attendance is good and even where it is not, there is not likely to be a greater number of the community gathered to hear God's word at any time during the week than at the Sunday celebration. But is this word coming across from the pulpit? Where it has been possible to initiate some preparation of the theme to be preached on among ordinary members of the community, and sometimes also a feed-back afterwards, the force and direction of the words spoken can be more immediate to the listeners. It is also necessary to remember that the preacher is very small fry in a world dominated by the voice of radio and the picture-voice of TV. For anyone who has been submitted to the ruthless editing of a producer it becomes clear how possible it is, without criticism and producing, just to bumble on.

As an extension of this preparation, it can be very useful for a group to prepare liturgies for certain seasons of the year. Normally, in my mind, the teaching periods are between October and Christmas, and between New Year and Easter, with a small possibility also between Pentecost and Trinity Sunday. At these points, if there are people prepared to study the weekly readings, to think and pray over what will be 'featured' say during Advent or Lent, there can be link-up with the teaching theme. And there can also be co-operation from schools, confirmation classes and so on, where paintings, posters and other illustrations can be produced as part of the class learning, and shared with the Sunday preaching in the wider community. They can be placed in church for all to see and learn from, as what I refer to as a modern equivalent of stained glass.

The importance of the Sacraments
The more rural existence of earlier centuries led to a closer celebration and awareness of both the seasons of the year and the ages of human beings. I have already spoken of the importance of parents being involved in preparation for their children's baptism, when this is celebrated at an early age. It is equally important to celebrate other sacraments as a parish community and a family occasion. If

children are initially brought into a real community which is wider than a family clique, there is every reason why all later involvement should be at the same level.

Immediate questions, which are being approached differently in different areas, are the age for a young person to be confirmed and to receive holy communion; and connected with this, whether confirmation and holy communion should be joined. The Roman Catholic practice has long been to bring a child at the age of seven or even six to holy communion, and to leave confirmation till somewhat later. Present practice is tending to continue the holy communion custom, while pushing confirmation more into the teenage period. It is certainly worth considering whether a way forward for other churches is through the earlier admission to holy communion.

The approach to holy communion in this situation is less child orientated and more family orientated, because parents are faced with their responsibility. There is more need for the young people to take responsibility for themselves in teenage confirmation, in emerging self-awareness and growth to adulthood. The build-up to confirmation here is aided by small groups led by an adult, meeting out of school hours; by days and weekends away; and by some introduction of the young people to work within the local community. Ideally, there is also a follow-up scheme for further involvement after the sacrament has been received, so that the gift of the Spirit flowers in both prayer/worship and service.

The theme of service can be very fruitful for the young people. (It can also reactivate the social conscience of the parents, relatives and neighbours, if they are centred in the toils of their everyday struggle to exist, to keep pace with inflation and the Joneses.) This in turn can lead on to the development which I have already mentioned of pre-marriage training. It is important to stress it again here, because of the central character and importance of the family in Christian living and renewal.

There has been laughing reference in the churches to those who are 'three-wheelers', that is those who come three times to church in a lifetime, and are each time carried: in baptism, in marriage and in death. But I want to underline the importance of these three occasions. Each should be prepared for—yes, even death. On the occasion of sacraments people are often brought together into church who seldom come otherwise. Not only can the immediate participants be involved in some pre-sacramental instruction and training, but on the occasion itself, a considerable opportunity is opened for leading, warming and instructing reluctant churchgoers, who may have only come to scoff, but may remain to pray. And this is even more possible during terminal illness and on the occasion of death. Here *par excellence* are events which affect the life of the community. Rather than hiding death and pretending it does not happen, families and neighbours can be drawn in beforehand, during sickness. On the occasion of the funeral, each person comes with a memory, a loss, and a question about his or her personal future, even a hope or a despair. Such moments may be validly taken as God's merciful love working to give us a glimpse of him. For we are all imperfect and we need a nudge now and then from God to renew us and open us to the future. This imperfection and the way it develops towards perfection are beautifully set before us in a sermon by Professor G. W. H. Lampe delivered just a few weeks before his own death:

> We are always on the way, almost growing up. I am not speaking of moral improvement or intellectual developments so much as of the constant incompleteness and rudimentary state of our response to the outreach towards us of God—which involves our capacity to love and to respond to love in other people, mediating the love of God. All that really matters most in life is always deficient in us. We cannot possibly think that communion with God, that by which we truly live, is ever full, complete and satisfying. That communion is what St Paul was talking about when he spoke of our inward man being renewed day by day. Renewal comes, or at least we experience renewal, in a very rudimentary way, and in fits and starts, however long we live this life. The people who are most conscious of its imperfection are the greatest of the saints. So, at the heart of our life there is unfulfilled hope, a promise and an assurance of the transformation of ourselves into the image of God in which, potentially, we have been created. That transformation cannot be completed in these few years of life; and if those years are all that there is for us, such glimpses of God as we now have are like a spring time without a summer to follow. Here is real ground for fear, and we need trust and hope as our preparation against it.
>
> (*Epworth Review*, September 1980)

Without overemphasizing the loss or the dread, a celebration can be deeply prayerful, full of hope and joy and the sense of resurrection, and a real new vision for even the most hardened members of the congregation.

Openness and sharing in the community

What has been said so far about the local community has tended to centre it upon the Eucharist and the other sacraments in rather a 'churchy' way. If this were all, then it would be a wrong emphasis and it would tend to further that kind of cliquish, narcissistic attitude which I have already opposed. Far from promoting this, the outcome of such suggestions as I have made should be greater communication between the members of the parish community, which will hopefully begin to look and spread outwards, rather than becoming in-turned. If it does not, something is wrong somewhere.

Again and again, the point must be made that the Church is bigger than the members who come to church. The churchgoers can feel self-righteous and want to exclude the non-churchgoers, but this attitude must be broken down, because it is not for each of us to make judgments; we little know the working of another person's heart, nor do we know the circumstances which lead to a certain way of life. It is of the essence of communion with God in deep prayer that we learn to love one another in such a sense as thinks well no matter what.

One aspect of this is that all renewal, like all religion, is for human beings. We are not made to fit religion. And that means that there is room for a wonderful variety, which is loved by God, but can be very tiresome for a community which would like to rope every individual into certain defined limits, ways of worship, and activity. It is more likely to be our own inadequacy, our intolerance, our anger or our hurt pride if we spend much of our time complaining at others for not following the way of prayer, worship or churchmanship which *we* see to be right. Being myself bad at achieving the balance, I chide myself often at my own lack of flexibility, lack of acceptance of a different way from my own. I wonder if I will ever learn.

There will always be those quiet ones who will not be involved; those lonely ones to whom others must go out; those shy ones who

69

do not readily put in a word in a prayer group or discussion; those contemplative ones who are more than they do. Each one in his or her own way adds something to the variegated pattern of Catholic and Christian living, if each can be appreciated, and if each can gain and give something.

We have to be aware of the appearance we give to strangers or those who feel 'outside'. Are we a community or a clique, are we open or shut? One day, a Roman Catholic man from Dominica in the West Indies said to me about a certain church, that he would never go there again. I asked why, and he said, he went at eight o'clock every Sunday morning and no one would sit beside him, because he was black. I suggested he might have got it wrong. He said that it was quite clear they would not sit beside him because he was black. I said it might be because he was a Roman Catholic. He was astonished, saying they were all Roman Catholics. I then made the point, which is not altogether a caricature, that no Roman Catholic sat beside another at eight on a Sunday morning if they could avoid doing so; and indeed they would normally get as far away as possible and preferably behind a pillar!

Such a question of openness and sharing applies not only as regards people of different racial background; it applies also as regards young people, the disabled, old people, and various minority groups who can feel unwanted. It is precisely here that much of the change of heart, the change of general attitude must be effected if the breadth and depth of the love of Christ is to be felt in the community at large. I remember a very dear and holy old priest whose constant refrain when faced with any idea which he considered new was, 'It has never been our custom.' How often such a phrase could be used to cover up the unwillingness of a small group within a parochial congregation to admit fresh air, the wind of change, into either the form of service, the music, the accommodation of young interest, or even the use of church property for youth activity.

Every parochial establishment should be prepared, as an act of spring cleaning, to have a re-examination of everything in its life and being from personnel to pews, and from church decoration to times of services, from involvement with the housebound to involvement in homelessness.

Chapter 6

FREE TIME

The sacrament of the present moment

Every minute of our lives is free time. It does not always seem to be so but our belief is that we have been made free by God who created us. Of course, anyone can point out that there are limits to my freedom; some are imposed by my nature (I cannot fly like a bird), some by my age (I can no longer jump like a ten year old). There are other conditionings which come within society, like being born in a particular country, at a particular time in history, gaining a certain education and so on.

Many trained in psychology will challenge this assertion of freedom, and it is not my purpose here to debate freedom. Rather I am simply making the point that there is no sense in the whole doctrine and following of Christ unless I am to some extent free to say 'yes' or 'no'. Much that has emerged at the end of the last century and throughout this century throws some light on freedom, motivation and influences upon the individual. But when all this has been thought about and taken into account, if we read the Scriptures we find statements about freedom in the Old and New Testaments which teach that we have some freedom of choice.

Christ said that he had come 'to proclaim liberty to captives'. Some psychologists may consider we are all captive no matter which way we turn. Christians would normally accept that they are partly captive, needing the release which is set forth in the Good News of Jesus Christ, and which has to be accepted freely by each one of us.

The freedom Christ teaches is fulfilled for us in our freely choosing to follow him—this is what truly sets us free. He himself shows what this means when he freely chooses to live according to the will of his Father. This will is love, and our response to love is to take

71

to ourselves the living out of the three loves already mentioned, love of God, self and neighbour.

In other words, by choosing freely to follow Christ, though we are technically free to opt out of such following at any time until the moment of death, we do in a sense, temporally at least, limit our own freedom.

The Catholic Church does not have the certainty of personal salvation *now* which characterizes other more fundamentalist teaching. The Catholic is certain of God's will to save, certain of God's power to save, and certain too of Christ's redemptive work culminating in his death on the cross. But the Catholic believes that the delicacy of God's love and sensitivity towards the people whom he has created and loves is to leave each person free either to accept and continue acceptance day by day, or to go off at a tangent of mistaken freedom, which is self-indulgence.

This reality leads to wide differences in the way of life of Catholics. Many have lived outstanding and even heroic lives in the strict desert or monastic asceticism, or working poorly and tirelessly in the world for the love of Jesus Christ. Others, remaining Catholic in name, have used their freedom for unjust purposes, sexual depravity, extortion, fraud, killing and many other evils. It is for the individual Christian to realize the freedom, to take possession of that freedom, and to live it out according to God's will: 'In his will is our peace.' We do not always believe that and we can chase ephemeral goals, but the reality of Christian living is in the acceptance and living out of what the great spiritual guide of the eighteenth century, de Caussade, called 'the sacrament of the present moment'.

Catholic Renewal, by heightening and deepening the sense of the spiritual in daily life, has an important part to play in recreating in more and more people's minds and hearts the reality of Jesus' promise: 'I am with you always, to the close of the age' (Matt. 28:20).

Are we geared to free time?

It is interesting to me to look at the life of Jesus Christ as we see it set out for us in the Gospels. According to the general interpretation, Jesus did little of any account until he was about the age of thirty.

72

He may have helped his mother in the house. He may have learnt from Joseph, and helped him in his work. We do not know.

Then about the age of thirty and for some two or three years, he moved about gathering followers, preaching, healing. Again we do not know day by day how his time was given, but we know at least two things. Much of his time was occupied with people, either those coming for healing or for instruction, or those whom he had chosen. Also we know that he used to go away by himself and with his close friends to be alone, away from pressure.

In the world at large, and even more especially in those parts of the world dominated by a Protestant ethic, work has become almost part of the dignity of mankind, rather than a burden. Yet in saying this it is clear that while there has been insistence virtually on the right to work, there has also been the contrary cry against the degradation of work, and pressure for shorter working weeks and greater freedom for those working. Meanwhile, the actual vigour at work has varied a great deal, with much less sense among many workers of the value of good work.

Now we are at a stage in history when there is a new revolution in technology. It seems unlikely that employment will be full again at the pitch we have known, no matter what party is in power. Other methods have to be thought about and perhaps other values have to be asserted or reasserted. This is a time when the Church has a very special opportunity to gear herself in philosophy and practical example to a new vision of the possibility and purpose of men and women in this world.

In an interesting passage on the Sabbath, Harvey Cox points out:

> All religions must cope with the apparent contradiction between a vision of reality as ultimately changeless and one that contains contrast, opposition and change. In the Bible the key terms are not 'being' and 'energy' but 'creation' and 'rest'. Viewed in this light, the idea of Sabbath is not naive or primitive at all. It is a highly sophisticated philosophical notion. It postulates an ultimate force in the universe which is not just passive and changeless but which acts and is acted upon. Yet it affirms what most religions also say about the ultimate: it is eternal and perfect. Sabbath links God and world and human being in a dialectic of

action and rest, of purposeful doing and 'just sitting'. The seventh day is holy to Yahweh, and one keeps it holy not by *doing* things for God or even for one's fellow human beings. One keeps it holy by doing nothing.

(Harvey Cox, *Turning East*. Simon and Schuster, New York, 1977)

Cox goes on to enlarge upon how the Sabbath really is the biblical equivalent to meditation, nurturing a kind of awareness which is like the Buddhist 'mindfulness'. Now the Sabbath as such is rather discounted in our civilization, and in its place we have introduced a lot of activity, with many people working overtime, seven days a week if they can—almost as though they feared inactivity.

I am drawn to think that the Church herself has fallen into the same trap of measuring work for God by activity of one sort or another. This is not only among the clergy, but also among the ordinary faithful. It seems that, harking back to the first chapter of this book, there are very many who write off stillness and 'doing nothing' in contemplation; many others pray actively but have never been introduced to the possibility of silence; yet others are simply uninterested in anything except action, and have no time for prayer of any sort.

Meanwhile there has been quite an amount of propaganda work done by purveyors of Transcendental Meditation and this has co-incided with considerable interest among younger Europeans and Americans in assorted approaches to meditation, particularly in various forms of Eastern mysticism. Where Christians have been available as guides to contemplative prayer, there have been some remarkable developments. But I am put in mind of an occasion when I was leading a mission at Birmingham University a year or two ago. After one talk when I had spoken of contemplation and mentioned *The Cloud of Unknowing* a student came to talk to me. He was a graduate from Malaysia. His question simply was could I tell him where in England he could go to find people teaching the kind of prayer he had read about in *The Cloud of Unknowing* and heard me mention. To be truthful (and it may be my ignorance) I was at a loss to give him much direction as to where he could go! Would you have had some addresses?

74

Our belief in free time
Our use of free time

If we once gear ourselves towards the notion that free time is positively good, there are some considerations we shall have to take into account. In the first place, it will mean that we have to preach, and enjoy, the virtue and the freedom of living at a reduced standard. We have become enmeshed in the professional, trade union and materialist concept that living standards must go up each year. We must now adjust, and help others to adjust, to the fact that for many in this world, including ourselves, there will be a reduction of living standards. It is to be hoped that this will develop levelling up in poverty areas, so that all people in high as well as low income brackets face change. Rather than this being a horror and a reason for interminable strikes, we should be strong to stress the positive advantages which accrue from freeing ourselves from the treadmill of constantly battling onwards in the material—and to what?

In saying this, let us not be ridiculous where there is obvious injustice and where poverty is degrading. But equally, let us be clear, at lots of different levels of society in the present day, that followers of Jesus Christ have a duty and a privilege of standing *with* as well as *for* the oppressed—not simply 'doing good' out of a surplus, or preaching for the poor from a position of financial security.

Jean Vanier, whose father was Governor General of Canada, gave up all he might have been and done to work with a totally new concept of being day-in-and-day-out with people who are classed by society as mentally handicapped. After years of experience living in this way, Jean made this prophetic statement that all of us should meditate:

> When you are rich, when you have a name, when you have friends or when you are a member of a respected group, you are never really oppressed. When in difficulty, simply make a telephone call and everything is fixed. I know this myself. I've never been really poor because I have enough friends and contacts. When you have no friends, when you are an immigrant and you speak the language badly, you are quickly oppressed, for you cannot defend yourself. This is true of the mentally deficient, the sick and handicapped, the prisoners, and all those who have no

voice. They are the oppressed ones and they are numerous in our society. There are many without work, with no security, living off meagre wages, living day by day in unbearable situations of fear and anxiety, with sick children and other dependents. We all know these situations. Each of us has met them. They are in the cities. They are all around us. But what is frightening is that the disciples of Jesus so often live in comfort. On which side of the road is Jesus? On which side of the road are his disciples? Are they on the same side? You can be sure that the first question that is always brought up in any situation when one is talking with people who are worried about faith in Jesus is the question of finance. Who has the money? What image am I giving of Jesus and of his mystical Body? Isn't it a terrible thing that the Poor One, the Crucified One, is thought to be with those who have surrounded themselves with comfort?

(Jean Vanier, *Followers of Jesus* Gill and Macmillan 1976, p. 57)

Jean Vanier seized the concept that all time was free, and has given himself and all that free time to being with the mentally handicapped. If you visit him or any one of the world-wide chain of settlements which he has established in different countries you will immediately know that time is not free in the sense which the ordinary person in the world means by free. But the freedom is there in that all those who work alongside Jean have freely given themselves and their time.

I think that most of us are inhibited from thinking or believing that we are free, and that our time is free. We tend rather to be caught up in a web of un-freedom. There are so many obligations, so many commitments, so many bills to be paid, taxes to be met, duties to be covered that there is a kind of chain-gang existence lived by very many, if not by most people. My submission is that Christians have every reason to live and to preach the breaking of the rat race, the end of the chain-gang, the liberation of ordinary people from the tyranny of materialistic happiness, which is really no happiness.

But in order that this should be possible, it is necessary that some Christians, wherever they are in society, should begin to live deliberately at a lower standard than they have been living, than they are accustomed to. A long time ago, the unfortunate and perhaps maligned Marie Antoinette is supposed to have said in reference to the food shortage in Paris, 'If they can't have bread, let them eat cake.' We can use this remark (rightly or wrongly attributed) to focus ourselves on the way we live, our standard. Are we as it were living on cake, when following Christ's example of poverty strongly suggests a 'bread' rather than a 'cake' standard? Often when I say or write this people respond by asking me to give a concrete example of what I mean about lowering our standards. But how can I really? You see it is not just knocking off a number of cigarettes, or not drinking so much, or eating a little less. It is something much deeper than that, which is involved with a change of heart, a change of outlook or attitude, but which in its interior revolution leads to living a simpler way, being less materialistically demanding, and gradually to working in the world for love of Christ and not for personal gain.

This is part of the difficulty. We can try to change ourselves and our outlook; but much of the change is not our doing, it is St Paul's 'spiritual revolution', as the Jerusalem Bible renders it. St Paul stresses: 'Be renewed in the spirit of your minds and put on a new nature created after the likeness of God in true righteousness and holiness.' This 'spiritual revolution' has to seize us in our guts as a Francis was seized or any one of the numerous army of men and women down the ages who have left all to follow Jesus. But it will not necessarily have the drama of Francis, because the new life may have to be lived out just where you are here and now—and that can be much harder, because it demands that there is change within the old pattern. There is something much more evidently clear-cut and decisive where a break can be made from the work environment, home and obligations, and a journey taken into the desert of a monastic or religious life. What I am suggesting is that within the ordinary home, the ordinary business life, the family, employment or unemployment, the new spirit of freedom in God has to make the change. And for this to be a continuing 'spiritual revolution', there will need to be support from the living Church.

The freedom of young people
Over the past twenty years or so, I have been involved in university work and in parochial work. In the former, I was immediately

alongside men and women in their late teens and early twenties. It was impossible to be with them and not to be impressed by the ability and generosity of large numbers. There were always those who were lost, needing moral, spiritual and psychological support; there were those who drifted. But the overall feel was of youth, energy, zeal and a willingness to serve others in a cause or in the reality of deprivation. Since coming into the parochial situation eleven years ago, I have had invitations to go back to the university scene for talks, missions and so on. Though the scene has changed, there is still the vigour and the openness to give. What I have found is that this exists also at the parochial level. Not only do young people move from very ordinary parish schooling and life into university, but there is always a vibrant local concern and action. These young people have ideas; they have energy. Often it is the older group who block their initiative. It is for all of us to open doors and windows so that they can grow and develop in service. There are many who never go educationally further than school but have an immense amount to give locally. There are also young people who after university are anxious to try to work for others and like the idea of joining the kind of open community setting which has been my way of life over the years.

I say this not out of self-glorification, but because I am quite sure that there is a large reservoir which is untapped. Taizé has caught its spirit and to some extent harnessed its energy, but there are many, many young people who are asking aloud or in violent reaction for some lead and guidance towards use of their time, their free time, which is theirs to give. So often those who pick them up and literally 'use' them are sects and organizations which, though not always roaring, are reminiscent of the devil who 'prowls around like a roaring lion, seeking some one to devour' (1 Peter 5:8).

By the time this is published a number of things may have happened. It is entirely probable that unemployment will have reached an even higher level; there is every likelihood that there will have been more acts of violence in urban areas, directed by white elements against Asians and West Indians, while there will also have been reactions from young West Indians especially, but also Asians, against both police and property. The people in the middle will be the police. There is no doubt that there is a ferment among young people, which is largely exacerbated by the social

78

scene of unemployment, free time with nothing constructive to do, frustration with society, and hostility to the symbols of law and order, the police. At the same time, certain factions will be doing what they can to rouse bitterness and violence.

Though it may already be too late to be effective, the churches have a serious responsibility to pray and work their way towards some planning of new ways and means of canalizing energy, irritation and potential violence towards positive goals—with all the authority and power of the word of God. This may mean standing in the face of much established thought and being prepared to alienate some of the faithful who are likely to be as established as anyone. And I do not believe it can be done unless there is a change of heart among leaders which will strengthen them to help all levels of society towards justice and peace.

It may be the older and the middle-aged who have the power in a political sense at the moment. But there is a tremendous power among the young, and it is for their minds and hearts that Christians must aim. And young people must be involved in the movement of renewal—which must have strength and conviction and plenty of challenge.

The priesthood of the people

In a wonderful, memorable and often quoted passage, St Peter wrote of the people of God: 'You are a chosen race, a royal priesthood, a holy nation, God's own people, that you may declare the wonderful deeds of him who called you out of darkness into his marvellous light. Once you were no people but now you are God's people; once you had not received mercy but now you have received mercy' (1 Peter 2:9–10).

At the beginning of this chapter I stated that all time is free time. Whether believing or non-believing everyone is encompassed by God's love. But looked at from another angle, once we are baptized, all time is Christ's time. Young, middling or old, we are one and all en-Christed through baptism. There is never any time when we are not en-Christed, even when we deliberately remove ourselves, because we cannot totally escape the love of God. I had a priest friend who told me that when he was working in a certain parish, the parish priest would stand in the pulpit on the Sunday before my friend went on holiday, and he would say to the congregation, 'Fr. X is going on holiday tomorrow, but do not forget there is no holiday from God.' Just as there is no holiday from living, no holiday from the married state, no holiday from ordained ministry, there is no holiday from the 'royal priesthood' of baptism.

Looked at in this way, we have the kaleidoscopic variation between freedom and commitment, where we are free in Christ because we are caught in Christ.

The Catholic tradition has generally stressed the central position of 'the priest', and left others, 'the laity', in a very secondary role. However, this has now begun to change, and if there is to be true growth throughout the Church, in every branch and age group, vested interests will be faced with a shock to their constitution. For the task laid down by St Peter, 'That you may declare the wonderful deeds of him who called you out of darkness into his own marvellous light', is your task and my task from baptism and confirmation, not only for those who are also in the ordained ministry.

Now, this is hard for the ordained priest, if he has been led to feel he is supreme leader. There are those among us like myself who have lived in the transition and are still doing so. The erosion of 'power' is unsettling and a threat. Nevertheless, I am quite convinced that there is no way forward unless the ordained priesthood willingly accepts the immense power and effectiveness of the 'royal priesthood', with encouragement, teaching and openness.

The ordained priest, the full time parish worker, the deaconess or religious brother or sister have the freedom of a dedicated commitment, but they should not be in it for personal gain, advancement or pride. Easily said. But those of us committed in this way should examine our consciences. God would not want us to usurp the work and charge given to the 'royal priesthood'.

There are very few works, actions, ministries which are exclusive to 'the priest'. He is minister of the Eucharist, he administers some of the sacraments such as baptism, confession, marriage and anointing. But in the past, lay men and women have heard each others' confession, and indeed there are many today who are to all intents and purposes bringing the healing power of Christ to sinners by their listening, counselling and absorption of guilt. This is not sacramental absolution, but it is a reconciliation effective in itself in the relation of person to person in Christ, which can as necessary be later presented to a priest. Similarly, in teaching the gospel, in counselling for marriage, in preparing for Holy Communion or for death, the ordinary person has a far bigger part to play than is generally accepted.

The scale of involvement and the scope of involvement must be studied both in clerical and lay circles, and between the two, so that the full potential emerges.

One of the intense joys of my own ministry has been the emergence of 'little people', who previously felt unworthy to say or do anything, but have now come forward to take Holy Communion to their sick friends, to read a bible service with them; to share instruction of their children in preparation for first Holy Communion; to be open to the thought of suffering and death, and so to help forward a dying member of the family, while consolidating the faith and joy of all the rest of the family. Over and above this, there are simple and ordinary boys and girls, men and women, who have become aware that they are witnesses and they can speak of Jesus, of belief, of salvation and of hope and joy.

The field is white for the harvest. The labourers are few, partly because it has not been explained that the Lord wants everyone to help; partly because those in charge are jealous of others helping; partly because we are all naturally lazy and diffident, and so on.

The way ahead is so long and so wide that it must involve more and more 'workers' if it is to be made smooth and straight for the Lord, and for people who are seeking the Lord. In the end, the preaching of the gospel is simple and not complicated. But it implies instruction, living and commitment, all of which we should be united in providing as Church and community.

Epilogue

JESUS CHRIST, BREAD BROKEN FOR THE NEW WORLD

Jesus Christ is the name of a human being born into this world nearly two thousand years ago. He lived, he was beaten, he was broken, he was put to death. His purpose was to love. He loved. He loves. His love forgives, heals, restores, enlivens, kindles a response of love.

What Jesus Christ has done is set out by an extraordinary man of this century:

> Forgiveness breaks the chain of causality because he who 'forgives' you—out of love—takes upon himself the consequences of what you have done. Forgiveness, therefore, always entails sacrifice.
>
> The price you must pay for your own liberation through another's sacrifice, is that you in turn must be willing to liberate in the same way, irrespective of the consequences to yourself.
>
> (Dag Hammarskjöld, *Markings* Faber 1964.)

The Eucharistic Congress which took place at Lourdes in July 1981 had as its theme: 'Jesus Christ, bread broken for the new world'. Though the numbers who attended were not very great, the spirit was; the gathering was both international and interdenominational. Discussing aspects not only of Eucharist but also of world affairs, the consensus was that the world of today and tomorrow urgently needs the full energy of the Church of Jesus Christ, if there is to be any constructive coming together and building in newness, justice and peace.

These are fine sentiments! Where will they lead? What hope is there that they will mature and be fruitful for God?

In the same way, with all the talk and thought and writing about renewal in the Church of England, or indeed in the whole Church of Jesus Christ, is there really a total commitment to unity, so that the Church may speak with one voice, witness with one life, suffer, be broken and rise again in the unity of love?

The challenge at the end of this small book is very simple. Jesus Christ was prepared through living to be betrayed and to be broken and to be put to death—broken for the new world.

Just how much is any church leader or indeed lay member of any denomination prepared in forgiveness to sacrifice? Is there any real opening, offering and sacrifice at the various levels which will break the chain of causality? Are you, the reader, prepared to let go of something you have held dear in belief or practice, because you believe that the overriding necessity, within fidelity to truth, is forgiveness and love?

After century upon century of insistence upon the *'filioque'* in the Nicene Creed, Pope John Paul II was prepared to drop it during the Pentecost celebrations in 1981, as a gesture to the Eastern Orthodox visitors to Rome. Can he, can the whole Roman Catholic Church and the Church of England really drop this doctrinal formulation, this statement of faith which has sown such seeds of disruption down the centuries? And if this is possible, can we also, Pope, Archbishop, Patriarch and common people make a further leap, and join together in Eucharist?

Do we want to? Do we dare to? Can we break the chain of causality? When the first astronaut stepped onto the moon it was one small step. For mankind it was a gigantic achievement. For mankind, the ecclesiastical bars to sharing the Eucharist before there is total unity are being argued interminably while not only Rome but the whole world approaches a burn-up.

Who has the courage? Who has the forgiveness? Who has the humility? Who has the love to sacrifice in order to liberate 'irrespective of the consequences to yourself'?

COME LORD JESUS!

Oliver

and bless all those
known to you and
revealed to me

by John